WINNING CRAPS FOR THE SERIOUS PLAYER

The Ultimate Money-Making Guide!

A NOTE ON THE 25 WINNING STRATEGIES

In addition to all the playing and strategy tips in this book, there are 25 complete winning strategies. For easy reference, you'll see these numbered in order from 1 through 25 in the table of contents.

WINNING CRAPS FOR THE SERIOUS PLAYER

The Ultimate Money-Making Guide!

J. Edward Allen

CARDOZA PUBLISHING

Cardoza Publishing, publisher of **Gambling Research Institute** (GRI) books, is the foremost gaming and gambling publisher in the world with a library of more than 75 up-to-date and easy-to-read books and strategies.

These authoritative works are written by the top experts in their fields and with more than 5,000,000 books in print, represent the best-selling and most popular gaming books anywhere.

1st Edition   *June 1993*
2nd Edition   *June 1997*

Libray of Congress Catalog Card No: 96-71756
ISBN:0-940685-74-4

CARDOZA PUBLISHING
P.O. Box 1500 Cooper Staion, New York, NY 10276
Phone (718)743-5229 • Fax (718)743-8284
E-Mail: CardozaPub@aol.com

Write for your free catalogue of gaming books,
advanced strategies and computer games.

TABLE OF CONTENTS

1. INTRODUCTION

Craps! Of all the games the casino offers, craps is far and away the most exciting. There's non-stop action, with betting allowed at all times, on each roll of the dice. It's certainly the game preferred by those who want fast action, and the chance to win enormous sums of money in the shortest period of time.

In the other games, in order to win big, you've got to bet big. You can't go to the blackjack table with $100 and expect to win $10,000. If you double your money, you've done well. If you triple your bankroll, hey, you're a big winner. But in craps, you can take that $100 and with a good run of the dice come out of there with $10,000 in an hour. I've seen it done any number of times. That's what's so great about the game. The action is continuous, and when the dice are hot, so are the winnings. Money multiplies quickly and it's as if you're coining it in your own private mint. We'll show you how to do it - how to make the big score.

Although craps is a popular game, it's popularity is limited by ignorance. Many gamblers avoid the game because they don't understand it. They see the layout with all its possible wagers and they freeze, not knowing what to do. Yet the game is simplicity itself. The layout showing the potential wagers will be discussed in full in this book. You can avoid most of the bets, which give the casino too big an advantage. We'll show you the best bets with the lowest house edge.

And the edge is low in craps. If you bet intelligently, as we will show, you will have most of your wagers out there at less than 1% in favor of the house. Many of these bets will be at .06% and sometimes lower. We'll guide you and take you step by step through the game.

For those of you with experience in the game, you'll be shown how to refine your game to win with the best betting methods available. Absolutely the best. You'll be giving the house the smallest advantage while reserving for yourself the most likely chance to make enormous sums of money. What could be better than that?

By the time you finish this book, you'll be a tough player feared by the house. Study this book carefully and you'll end up a winner.

2. CASINO PERSONNEL

Introduction

The casino operates and runs the craps game with its employees. The employees work for and are paid by the casino, but several of the employees you meet at the table will be on your side. They want you to win, and to win big. The reason for this is simple - winners generally **tip** or **toke** the dealers. So the dealers will be rooting for you. Other personnel at the table will be openly rooting against you. They don't get tips and they are there to do only one thing - protect the casino's bankroll.

No many players realize the paradoxical situation that exists at the craps table. It's as if two distinct forces are working against each other. One group wants you to win and one group wants you to lose. The smart thing, as we shall show, is to align yourself with the people who are hoping you win. It's in your best interest and theirs if you win.

Dealers

Every craps table in a casino is staffed by four dealers. You won't see four of them at any one time, just three, for three work the table while one is *on break*. Most of the time these dealers move around the table at intervals and take up different positions. One will be *on the stick*, while the other two will be standing on the opposite side of the table, servicing, if you will, the players. They are *on base*.

The dealers wear the uniform of the casino. Most casinos require their dealers to wear black and white - black pants and a white shirt, often with a black tie. The uniforms may vary from casino to casino. Some of the new houses which cater to the outlandish, will have their dealers dressing like clowns. It doesn't matter to you. What matters is the attitude of the dealers to you and their competency and honesty.

As mentioned, there are three active dealers. The one who handles the stick is known as *the stickman*. Let's see what his duties are.

The Stickman

This dealer holds a malleable stick made of wood. He uses the stick to gather in the dice used in the game and he controls an area of the table where wagers, known as **proposition bets**, are made by the players. Let us say for now that any bet the stickman controls isn't worth making. If you stop reading this book at this point, and simply digest this bit of advice, you've saved yourself tons of money.

We'll go into the proposition bets later. Let's for now just understand that these bets are under the stickman's control. When a proposition bet is won, he directs a standing dealer to pay it off. When the bet is lost, which is more often the case, he takes it off the betting area and keeps the losing bet or throws it across the table to a seated boxman.

The stickman also controls the dice. Usually anywhere from six to eight dice are in a small tray in front of him. When a new shooter gets ready to roll the dice, all the dice in the tray are pushed to the shooter. After the shooter selects two of them, the stickman, with his stick, pulls the remaining dice back to his domain and replaces them in the tray.

After the dice are rolled, it is the stickman's job to call out the roll. Suppose a 6 is rolled; the stickman will announce, *six*. If it's the first roll of the dice by the shooter, he will say *six, the point*. Sometimes stickmen jazz up the game with their patter.

Instead of simply calling out *six*, a stickman might say, *six, the juicy red six is the point*. A good stickman can energize a table and bring out more action from the gamblers there.

After the dice are rolled, bets are usually placed by various gamblers, and the stickman waits till all the bets are placed before returning the dice to the shooter with his stick. If the shooter sevens out, that is, loses his roll, the stickman will slide the dice back to himself, and place them in the cup, ready to be selected by the next shooter.

The Standing Dealers

In addition to the stickman, the other two members of the crew are the **standing dealers**. They are on the opposite side of the table, and are there to service the players. When a player comes to the table with cash, he gives the cash to the dealer, who immediately gives it to the boxman, who is seated between the standing dealers. The boxman counts the cash, verifies its amount with the player, and then tells the dealer to give the gambler the chips representing that amount.

Cash and Chip Transactions

The dealer may ask the player how he wants the chips. That is, in what denominations. Chips, also called **casino checks**, come in fairly standard denominations in casinos. The smallest are $1 chips, then $5, $25, $100 and $500.

Payoffs or bets less than a dollar are with ordinary US coins.

A player may want to break down a particular chip or chips during the game. For example, he or she might be holding a $100 chip and want to make smaller bets. The usual procedure is to ask the dealer to **change color**. The $100 chip will then be broken down into $5 or $25 chips or whatever denominations the player desires.

Exchanges between the dealer and player are never done hand-to-hand. This rule is in effect to prevent collusion and cheating. A player puts his cash on the table, and receives his chips on the table, then picks them up himself. If a bet is made, the same procedure follows - the chips are placed on the table by the player and then picked up by the dealer.

Bets and Payouts

The placing of bets is an important job of the dealer. A player can make several bets himself, but certain wagers, as we'll explain in the appropriate sections, must be made by the dealer. In that case, the chips are placed on the green (or other color) layout by the player with instructions to the dealer as to what wager to place. The dealer will then pick up the chips and make the appropriate bet or bets.

After the dice are rolled, if any payouts are to be made, the dealer will make the payouts. He will place the chips on the layout near the player, for the player to pick up himself.

If the roll creates losses for the bettors, the dealer will take away the chips, and stack them on the layout in front of him. Sometimes, if the losing bets are enormous, he might give the overflow to the boxman.

The usual procedure after a roll of the dice is for the dealer to collect and remove all losing bets first. Then he makes payouts to those who have won as a result of the roll.

If a proposition wager is won by the player, the stickman will direct the dealer to make the payout to the winning gambler.

There are two standing dealers at each table. One services one side of the table, while the other handles the other side. Usually an average table handles between twelve and twenty players when full, so each dealer will take care of six to ten players. A competent dealer can do this easily. Sometimes, on a crowded table, where the action is hot and heavy, and there are a multitude of bets out, the dealers will work at a slower and more methodical pace, to make certain they don't make mistakes. Sometimes a payout will be made to the wrong player in the heat of the game, but this rarely happens.

However, dealers are human beings and all human beings make mistakes. It is up to you to protect your interests at the table. When you make a bet, be certain that the dealer has made the correct wager for you. When you're due for a payout, make sure you get the payout. And check to see that is in the correct amount.

The Marker Buck

There is still another duty that the dealer has. At the outset of play before a shooter throws the dice for the first time, he is responsible for the **buck**, a round disk which usually has two sides and two distinct colors. As we shall see, once the dice are rolled a point may be established, which point number the shooter must repeat before a seven is rolled in order to win.

Before the point is established, the buck will be placed by the dealer in the Don't Come box next to the place numbers. The black side of the buck will be evident there, telling all players that no point has been established yet.

Any new player coming to the table can immediately see that this is the case just by looking for the buck.

One a point has been established, whether it is a 4, 5, 6, 8, 9 or 10, the buck will be turned to its white side and placed in the appropriate numbered box, so all players know immediately just what the point is, and any new players can see the point, and know that a roll is in progress.

After a shooter sevens-out and loses the dice, the buck is then moved back to the Don't Come box and placed on its black side, till the next shooter establishes a point.

The Boxman

Unlike the dealers and stickman, the **boxman** doesn't wear the house uniform. Instead, he is most likely to be dressed in a business suit or a sports jacket and pants, wearing a shirt and tie. His position at the table is between the two standing dealers. He is directly opposite the stickman.

The boxman's main duty at the craps table is to protect the bankroll of the casino. He is ever alert to chicanery, collusion or cheating on the part of the players or the dealers. During the action he remains seated. After the dice are rolled, he looks in one direction, and the stickman in another, in this way covering the table. He makes sure that the payouts to players are correct, and after a losing roll, that the chips are properly collected by the dealers.

The boxman sits tight and protects the stacks of chips under his domain, which are neatly piled up in front of him according to the various denominations. At an action table in a plush casino, he may have hundreds of thousands to protect in this way. That's his job.

Unlike the dealers, who chat with the players and are friendly souls, the boxman is usually a sour individual forever watching what is going on. Sometimes a boxman can be friendly also, but that's not what he's there for. He's not a P.R. guy. He runs the game and his decision in disputes between a player and a dealer is final. When there are disputes, if it's not a clear issue, he will generally give the benefit of the doubt to the player. Once. After that, he'll rule against the same player.

When a player brings cash to the table, the boxman will count the money and verify its amount and make certain that it's not counterfeit, and then tell the dealer to give the player chips covering that amount. The boxman **drops** the cash into a slot which leads to a **drop box** underneath the table. Cash may be bet by players, but no one is paid off in cash, just casino chips.

If the table is losing money to players, he will release some of the chips in front of him to dealers to facilitate their payoffs. If the players are losing, and chips are accumulating in front of dealers, he will take some of their stacks and put them under his control.

If he feels that the dice are running too hot, the boxman may examine the dice to verify that they're not phonies introduced by a cheat. Whenever a die or dice go beyond the table and land off the table, the boxman will examine them to verify that they're casino dice. Dice have a logo and number on them. He'll check these out before allowing them to go back into play.

The Floorman

This supervisory person stands in the area known as the **craps pit**. A casino will usually have an array of craps tables surrounding an inner space, known as the **pit**. The two end tables are parallel with each other, while the other tables are perpendicular to the end tables. Within that pit area stands the **floorman**.

Usually there is more than one floorman to service the area, especially if most or all of the tables are in operation. He also watches the game to make sure it's honest. By standing there he has a good view of the action. He watches the play and the casino bankroll. He observes the spectators, making certain none of them are thieves, stealing chips from the players' **rails**, the area where chips are held, while the action is hot and heavy.

The floorman wears a business suit or sports jacket and trousers. He will also be wearing a shirt and tie. He is usually more friendly with the players than is the boxman, for one of his jobs is to extend credit to players. In many casinos, players can establish a credit relationship with the house, so that they don't have to bring cash to the game. When a player has credit, he is introduced to the floorman who asks his or her name, and then verifies the credit arrangement through a computer or clerk in the pit. If the credit is satisfactory, the floorman will give the player a **marker** to sign. A *marker* is in essence, an IOU. After it is signed, the floorman will tell the boxman or dealer to give the player that amount in chips.

A floorman also has the option of giving a player various **perks**, ranging from a free room to meals or a free show in the casino theater. The floorman will work with guidelines established by the casino, and give the perks if they're warranted by the amount of action the player gives to the casino. By **action**, we mean the level and frequency of the player's bets.

For so much action, a free room, along with everything else, will be given to the player. For lesser action, a free meal may be offered. Or a free show. If a player makes a big score, the floorman will jump at the chance of inviting the winner to stay at the casino, with the hope that if he continues to play, he'll lose back the winnings.

The floorman may also be a kind of appeals judge if the player, after having a dispute with a dealer, is unhappy with the boxman's decision. The floorman will rarely overrule a boxman, but he may, at his discretion. Usually this will happen if he knows the player is a **premium player** or **high roller**, and he feels that giving in is a small price to pay for the gambler's action.

The Pitboss

Outranking the floormen and all other employees in the pit is the **pitboss**. He is the final arbiter of all that goes on in the craps pit. Whereas a floorman may be responsible for one or two tables, the pitboss is responsible for the entire action of all the tables. He will be wearing a business suit or the sports jacket and trousers, and many times the floorman will be mistakenly called a pitboss. But there'll only be one in command.

Usually a floorman can handle anything a player wants, but there may be times when a pitboss will be called in. A player may want more credit after his funds run out. Or he may want some special favor that the floorman can't give. Or whatever. The pitboss is the ultimate boss of the craps pit.

So there they are. The dealers will be rooting for you to win, for they want your tokes. The boxman will be wincing if you have a hot roll and pick up big money from the casino. The floorman has the power to do you some favors either big or small. The pitboss stands above it all.

The Stickman's Pattern

The stickman runs the game by keeping its rhythm going. He holds up the dice, till all bets are made and collected or paid off. He calls out the roll of the dice and announces winning and losing rolls. He also keeps up a nonending stream of talk, if he's a good stickman, one who can energize a game.

Before the opening roll, he will usually say, *get those bets down on craps, eleven, bet the Field.*

He calls out the roll, and usually has something to say about it. On the come-out, the initial roll of the dice, if it's an 11, he'll say *yo- leven, a winner on the passline. Bet that 11.*

If the roll is a craps, which loses for most players, he'll find something good in it, *craps, the deuce pays 30-1. Bet that deuce, bet the 12, bet any craps.*

A 7 on the come out calls for him to say *A winner! 7, a winner!*

In the private game of craps, there are many terms for the dice. *Eighter from Decatur,* means an 8. *Little Joe from Kokomo,* is the 4. *Boxcars* is the 12. The 10 is often called *Big Dick.* The 2 is known universally as *Snake Eyes.* Some call the six *Jiminy Sticks.*

But in the casino game, these colorful terms are dispensed with, so the stickman has to use his imagination. If a 6 is rolled, he might call it the *big, juicy 6.* The 9 is *center field,* since it is the middle number in the Field Bet.

The stickman wants you to bet the hardways, center or proposition bets favorable to the house. After the first roll of the dice when a point is established, he'll get on the hardways. *Bet those hardways, bring out the point.* If the point can be paired, he'll call for that particular hardway. *Bring out the 4, bet it hard.*

If a 4 is then rolled not as a pair, he'll call out, 4, *easy, bet it hard.*

In American casinos the imagery is rather staid, but in the Caribbean, a stickman will tell you to bet the Field. Why? *The farmer made his fortune in the field.* He'll call the 10 a *sunflower,* and also have expressive names for the other numbers.

I like to play at a table with a good stickman. He moves the game along, and his patter can be a lot of fun. Of course, it's more fun to win.

3. THE TABLE AND CRAPS LAYOUT

Introduction

The game of casino craps is played on a table with a felt covering. The felt covering has an imprint which is called the **layout**. The layout shows all the bets that can be made, but there are other bets not shown on the layout which are of extreme usefulness to the player. In the appropriate sections we'll cover them all.

The Table

The table is about the length of mid-sized American car, with a width under five feet. There is no set standard size; it depends on the casino. The flat part of the table which contains the layout, is surrounded for the most part by wooden sides which run the length of the table, except for several cut away spots. One spot is where the stickman stands, and directly across from him is another space for the seated boxman.

On the very top of the wooden sides are **rails**, which are cutaway grooves in the wood for the player's chips. These rails are cut to the exact size of the casino chips, so that they can be stored there while the gambler plays craps. It is up to the player to protect his chips and shield them with his body.

The players stand during the game. There are no seats though a handicapped person would probably be accommodated by a chair or stool. Everyone is standing except the boxman, who must look up to see the players and the dealers. Most tables will accommodate at least twelve players. However, some casinos have really big tables that may stand twenty gamblers at a time.

The height of the sides is approximately four feet, although this is not standard. Casinos may vary the height of their tables from that norm. It allows the players to stand comfortably and to handle their chips easily. It also permits them to look down at the action on the table.

On the inside of the sides, the table is padded with a soft substance, such as foam rubber, which not only deflects the thrown dice, but allows the dice to have a random roll after the sides are hit. Sometimes, interspersed among the foam rubber, there may be mirrors, for the convenience of the boxman and floorman, to make sure the game is run honestly, for the mirrors allow them to see several sides of the table at once.

That basically is the structure and purpose of the table. It is an enclosed area, so the dice are always on the table in front of the players and the employees of the casino.

The Layout

The flat part of the table, the surface, is covered with a felt cover on which are imprinted the bets that can be made by the players. As mentioned before, not all bets are printed there, but this is what we'll find when we come to a casino craps table, ready to play.

First of all, the layout may be of various colors, though green is the most common. Some casinos incorporate other colors to match their logo. Blue is next most common, and some have an eye-boggling red, extremely uncomfortable to look at and play on.

Dividing the areas are white lines. Some of the bets you can make are in yellow, others are in red or white, or still other colors. All this is immaterial. What is important is what bets can be made.

The following is a typical casino craps layout:

CRAPS LAYOUT

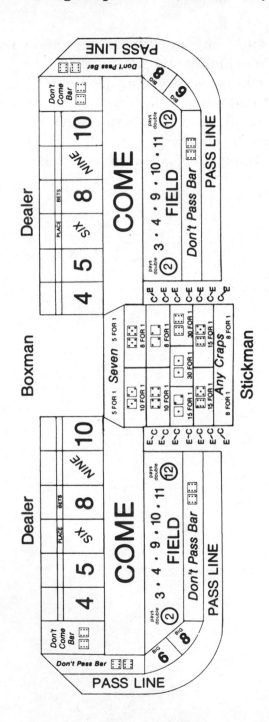

The first thing we notice is that there are three distinct areas. The two end sections are identical; the middle area separating them is distinctive.

Let's look at the two identical areas first. They are identical because players at either end of the table, serviced by a standing dealer, can make the same kinds of bets no matter where they stand.

The Layout - Pass-Line Bet

Although its space is relatively small, the most common bets made in craps are *pass-line* wagers. Notice how this area runs all the way from the proposition bets in the center to the end of the table. A great deal of action will center on that pass-line during the course of a session of craps.

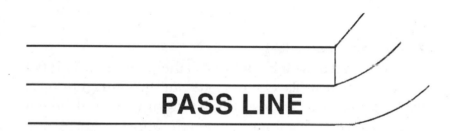

The Layout - Don't Pass Bet

Diametrically opposed to that wager is the ***Don't pass bet***. Although the odds are the same as the pass-line, it has few adherents, and little action. Therefore the space reserved for don't pass is much smaller.

Both pass-line and don't pass bets are made before the initial roll of the dice to establish a point. We'll discuss these bets thoroughly in the appropriate section. Note that with the don't pass bet area there is a printed statement *Bar 12*. This means that if you bet don't pass and the 12 is rolled at the outset, though the pass-line bettors lose, you don't win. It is a **push**, a standoff.

In some casinos the 2 is barred; no matter. Each of these numbers, 2 or 12, can only be made one-way with the dice. Those numbers are barred to allow the casino to have an advantage on don't pass wagers.

The Layout - Come Bet

A huge area, with big letters, is the *Come* box. This bet is a good one for players to make, but through ignorance, very few make it because they don't understand how it works. However, we'll show you in the appropriate section how to make use of this terrific bet, for it can make a lot of money for you while giving the casino a very, very small advantage.

COME

The Layout - Don't Come Bet

The opposite bet to the Come wager is *Don't Come*. It is a very small box indeed, stuck next to the number 4 box. This bet gets hardly any action, for again, players don't like to bet against the dice, and if they do, many don't understand the workings of a Don't Come wager. But we'll show you why this is a great wager for you at the appropriate time.

							Don't Come Bar
							⚅ ⚅

The Layout - Field Bet

Another big area on the layout is the *Field*. Notice that on the Field part of the layout are a group of numbers 2, 3, 4, 9, 10, 11 and 12, with both the 2 and the 12 being circled. If any of those numbers come up on the next roll of the dice and you've made a Field bet, you win. If the circled numbers come up, you may be paid 2-1 or even 3-1 depending on the casino.

It looks like a great bet with all those numbers to have on your side, but in reality it's not a good wager at all. The numbers missing from the Field bet, which cause the bet to be lost, make up the heart of the probable dice rolls. The Field bet is a favorite with novices, who enjoy getting a decision immediately after a roll, and don't really understand that there are much better wagers to be made on the craps layout.

The Layout - Big 6 and Big 8 Bet

The bets also take up a prominent place on the layout. If you bet either the Big 6 and Big 8 and that number repeats before a 7 is rolled, the bet is won, but at prohibitive odds. Like the Field wager, this bet attracts novices and people completely unfamiliar with the odds of craps. There are other ways to bet on the 6 and 8, as will be shown, giving the house 1/6 the advantage it enjoys on the Big 6 and Big 8.

The Layout - Place Bets

Next to the Don't Come box are a series of numbers 4, 5, 6, 8, 9 and 10. These are known as place numbers and its here that the buck winds up after a point is established on the first roll of the dice. If the first number rolled is a 5, for example, the buck will be placed by the dealer on the 5, showing that this is the point.

A gambler doesn't have to wait for the dice to roll a particular number in order to make a wager that this number will repeat. A player can bet on any of the numbers in the place number boxes at any time, by giving his or her chips to the dealer and asking that the bet be made. The odds vary on the particular number, all of which will be thoroughly explained in the appropriate sections.

The Layout - Come and Don't Come Bets

Also, any come or don't come wagers wind up here as well, in the place box area with the come wagers in the larger area of the number, while the don't come bets are put in the smaller top area. Note the line or lines separating the two areas on the layout.

The Invisible Free-Odds Bets

Those are the basic wagers that can be made on the sides of the layout. We left out an important bet that is not shown on the layout, and that is the free-odds bet, either with or against the dice. This will be thoroughly explained in the section covering each wager, and its comparative merit.

The Center Bets

Having given an overview of the two equal sides of the layout, we now come the center, the domain of the stickman. There are a multitude of wagers available here. There's the hardway wagers, the wager on the 7 and the 11, and so forth. We'll cover all these in detail, but for now the reader should understand one thing. None of these bets are worthwhile. They're all sucker wagers with prohibitive odds ranging from 9% and up in favor of the house. Why make these bets when you can make others that give the casino only 0.6% in its favor?

That covers the layout, as seen in practically all American casinos. Most of the bets presented are bad, but there are a few that are worthwhile. Once the reader knows which bets to make and which to avoid, he or she will be on the way to winning.

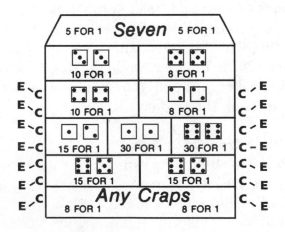

4. THE DICE COMBINATIONS

The Dice

The game of casino craps is played with two dice. Each die is a perfect cube, about 3/4 of an inch in width. The edges are sharp and pointed, and can do damage to an individual if thrown incorrectly and end up bouncing into someone's face.

Casino dice are bigger than the ordinary dice used in games like Monopoly or backgammon. Those games use smaller rounded dice. Casino dice usually have the casino's logo imprinted on them, as well as a coded number. Both are there for security. There are cheats who are facile at switching dice during play, and what the house wants is an honest game.

Sometimes, when a shooter is on a hot roll, that is, he's making winning numbers over a long period of time, the boxman may ask for the dice and examine them, to make certain that they are the real casino dice. Everytime a die or the dice are thrown off the table, they're examined as well by the boxman, for it is easy to switch the dice at that time.

To further secure the dice, they're made of a hard transparent plastic, which prevents them from being loaded with a weighted substance to ensure certain numbers coming up on the roll.

The Combinations

Since each die is a close to perfect cube having six sides, two dice in conjunction can hold 36 possible combinations (six combinations x six combinations).

The following are the numbers that can be rolled with two dice:

Dice Combinations

Number	Combinations	Ways to Roll
2	1-1	1
3	1-2, 2-1	2
4	1-3, 3-1, 2-2	3
5	1-4, 4-1, 2-3, 3-2	4
6	1-5, 5-1, 2-4, 4-2, 3-3	5
7	1-6, 6-1, 2-5, 5-2, 3-4, 4-3	6
8	2-6, 6-2, 3-5, 5-3, 4-4	5
9	3-6, 6-3, 4-5, 5-4	4
10	4-6, 6-4, 5-5	3
11	5-6, 6-5	2
12	6-6	1

Note the symmetrical curve of the numbers. The center is the 7, the most important number in the game. A 7 can be rolled no matter what number shows on any die; this is its' unique status. All other numbers are measured against the 7 to form the odds that govern the game of casino craps.

The Odds of the Point Numbers

In craps, certain numbers are called *point numbers*. These are the 4, 5, 6, 8, 9 and 10. From the above chart, we can see that the 4 and 10 can be rolled three ways. Since the 7 can be rolled in six ways, the chances of a 7 coming up before a 4 or 10 is repeated is 2-1. The 5 and 9 can be rolled four ways each; therefore the chances of a 7 being thrown before a 5 or 9 is repeated is 3-2. The 6 and 8 can be rolled the most ways of any point number - five each. The odds that a 7 will come up against these numbers is 6-5.

Those are the odds on the point numbers, all measured against the 7 in determining their correct odds.

The Odds of a Roll

Let's look at some other numbers. For example, a player can make a wager that the next roll of the dice will be an 11. If he wins, he'll be paid off at 15-1. But the correct odds are 17-1. That is calculated in the following way.

The 11 can be rolled in only two ways; a 5-6 or 6-5. There are thirty-six possible combinations. Therefore, the chances of rolling an 11 on the very next throw of the dice is 2 in 36, or 1 in 18, which translates to 17-1. If a player gets 15-1 for this bet, he is giving the house over 10% as its edge. If the payoff is at 15 for 1, which in reality is 14-1, then the house advantage is an astonishing 16.67%. That's why we say here and throughout the book - avoid the proposition bets.

Let's now reprise the odds. First of all, the chances of repeating a number before a 7 is rolled.

Number	True Odds Against
4 or 10	2-1
5 or 9	3-2
6 or 8	6-5

The odds of rolling an individual number that you can bet on with a proposition bet is as follows:

Number	True Odds Against
2 or 12	35-1
3 or 11	17-1
Any 7	5-1

If you understand these odds, you'll have an intelligent idea of what bets to make and what to avoid, and you'll have a better insight into the game of casino craps.

5. HOW THE GAME IS PLAYED

Getting Ready to Play

Let's start at the very beginning, so the game will be absolutely clear. We'll assume that a craps table has just opened for action, and a number of gamblers saunter up to the table to play casino craps.

The first thing the players will do is put down cash and exchange the cash with the dealers for casino chips. Once all the players have their chips, the stickman will pass the dice to the player to his left. Thereafter, the dice will move in an orderly fashion around the table, clockwise. Thus each player will have a chance to get the dice after the player to his right gives them up.

The first player, and any other player, may refuse to roll the dice. That's their privilege, and yours also. Some players are superstitious, some shy, some bet against the dice and don't want to bet against their roll. Whatever the reason, there's no stigma attached to refusing the dice.

But let's assume that the first player wants to roll the dice. He selects two from the half-dozen or so presented to him by the stickman. After he picks up two, the stickman will pull the rest back to him with his stick and place them in a tray made to hold the dice.

But before the game starts, bets have to be made. The most common wagers at this point will be pass-line and don't pass wagers. Those betting on the pass-line are wagering that the dice will win, or pass. Those betting on the don't pass line are betting that the dice will lose, or not pass.

These bets are made in the appropriate betting areas on the layout. They are made by the players, who put down chips themselves, without help from the standing dealers.

Other wagers can also be made at this time. There may be some bettors who will place chips on the Field or the Big 6 or Big 8. Others may make proposition bets, usually one-roll wagers such as betting that a 12 or 3 will come up on the next roll. These bets, along with the Field bets are **one-roll wagers**, either won or lost on the next toss of the dice.

The Come-Out Roll

After the bets are made, the **shooter** is ready to throw the dice.His initial toss is called the **come-out**. If he rolls a 7 or 11, he and all players who bet on the pass-line are immediate winners. They'll be paid even-money for their pass-line wagers.

All those who bet against the dice, by betting don't pass, are immediate losers. Their chips will be swept away by the standing dealers.

If on the first roll of the dice the shooter throws a 2, 3 or 12, he is said to have **crapped out**, for all of these numbers are **craps**. All pass-line bettors lose their bets immediately. The bettors who wagered on the don't pass, or against the dice, will win their bets if a 2 or 3 is rolled. A roll of the 12 will be considered a **push**, with neither the house nor the don't pass bettor winning or losing. In some casinos, the 2 may be **barred** instead of the 12. It is immaterial which is barred, for either can only be made in one way.

When any number other than a **point number**, which is a 4, 5, 6, 8, 9 or 10 is rolled on the first throw of the dice,

even though the shooter may have won or lost, he continues to hold the dice, and the very next roll is still considered
a come-out throw.

For example, if the first roll is a 7, the pass-line bettors
win and the don't pass bettors lose, and the dice are still
retained by the shooter. His very next roll is a come-out. If
he now throws a 3, even though the pass-line bettors lose
and the don't pass bettors win, he still retains the dice.

If he throws 4, 5, 6, 8, 9 or 10 now, then this number is
considered the **point number**. He must repeat this number
before a 7 shows on the dice, not only for the pass-line
bettors to win, but for the shooter to retain the dice.

Let's assume the shooter repeats the 6 before a 7 shows.
Having repeated the 6, then the very next roll after his
second 6 is a new come-out roll, with the same shooter
retaining the dice. Should he roll a 7, however, before
repeating the 6, then he is said to have **sevened-out**, and not
only do the pass-line bettors lose, but he also loses the dice.
The player to his left gets the dice and prepares for his first
come-out roll.

A shooter doesn't lose the dice unless he sevens-out. Of
course, he may relinquish the dice voluntarily at any time,
unless a point has been established and is still operative.
For example, suppose the shooter rolled an 8, and that's
the point. He can't now give up the dice. He must keep
rolling to either make the 8 or seven-out. If he makes the
8, he can now give up the dice. This is very rarely done.

But should the shooter seven-out, he has no choice. He
must relinquish the dice to the next shooter.

The come-out roll, together with the establishing of a
point, and either repeating the point or sevening-out, is the
very basic game of craps. However, the casino, in its
wisdom, offers a multitude of other bets to the casino craps
player.

6. THE BEST BETS

The Come-Out Roll - Reprised

Let's discuss the come-out roll, one more time, to make it perfectly clear. Whenever the first roll of the dice is other than a 4, 5, 6, 8, 9 or 10, no point has been established, and the next roll of the dice is still a come-out roll. For example, if the initial throw of the dice by the shooter is a 2, a craps, the shooter is said to have crapped out, but he still retains the dice, and his next roll is once more a come-out.

Let's assume he rolls a 3. He craps out again, but still retains the dice for yet another come-out roll. If he now throws an 11, this is a winner for those betting with the dice, but once more the shooter will have a come-out roll.

However, should he roll a 6 on the next roll, that 6 becomes the point number, and he no longer will have a come-out roll. Now, he tries to repeat the 6 before a 7 comes up in order to win. If a 7 comes up before the 6, then he loses, and relinquishes the dice. He is said to have **sevened out**, and a new shooter now holds the dice for his or her come-out roll.

The Pass-Line

This is the most popular of all the casino craps bets. A player betting on the **pass-line** is said to be **betting with the dice**, or betting **right**. The casino, which books all bets, doesn't care if the player bets with the dice or against the dice. It has an edge on all wagers except for one, the free odds bet, which will be discussed later.

For now, we will be involved with the pass-line wager. It is made before the come-out roll. After a point is established, there can be no pass-line wagers.

Here's how the bet works. You're at a craps table and a new shooter is about to throw the dice for his come-out roll. You want to bet with the dice. So you place your chips in the pass-line area of the layout, directly in front of you. Let's assume you bet $10, or two $5 chips there. Now the dice are thrown by the shooter.

If he throws a 7 or 11, it is an immediate win for you. The dealer will place $10 in chips next to your bet, paying you off at **even-money**.

If the shooter had thrown a 2, 3 or 12, this would have been an immediate loss, and your $10 would have been whisked away by the dealer.

Let's say that the first roll was a 7 and you won $10. You feel lucky and leave the full $20 on the pass-line.

The next roll of the dice is a 4. 4 is a point number and thus a point number has been established. The buck is moved to the 4 on the place numbers. Now, in order for you to win your pass-line wager, the 4 has to be repeated before a 7 is rolled. The odds against this happening, however, are 2-1. There are only three ways to make a 4 (1-3, 3-1, 2-2), while there are six ways to roll a 7.

Don't Pass Wager

When you bet **don't pass**, you're betting against the dice. The casino refers to you as a **wrong bettor**. This doesn't have anything to do with wrongdoing, it's just an idiomatic term used by the house and other players.

Most bettors, about 90% of them, bet with the dice. However, whether you bet with or against the dice, the odds are the same against you. If you make a simple line wager without laying odds, then the house enjoys a 1.40% advantage. If you lay single odds, the advantage is reduced to 0.8%. With double odds the edge drops down to 0.6%.

An Analysis of Pass-Line and Don't Pass Bets

Although the odds on both bets are practically identical, the pass-line bettor is in the superior position on the come-out roll. There are eight ways for him to win immediately and only four ways for him to lose at once.

The 7 can be made in six ways, and the 11 in two ways. This gives the pass-line bettor eight immediate ways to win. If the 2, 3 or 12 is thrown, he is an immediate loser. Since these numbers can be rolled only four ways, he is 8-4 (2-1) to win immediately if no point number is rolled.

However, once a point number is rolled and established, the odds switch to the don't pass bettor, If a 6 or 8, the most common point numbers, are rolled, the don't pass bettor now has a 6-5 advantage on his bet. A 5 or 9 gives him a 3-2 advantage, and a 4 or 10, a whopping 2-1 advantage.

These factors should be considered when betting either pass-line or don't pass. If you feel that a lot of points will be established and lost to a 7, then bet don't pass. If you feel that a lot of 7s and 11s will show on the dice and then points will be made, bet the pass-line.

Also, as we will show, you shouldn't limit yourself to just pass-line or don't pass bets with free odds added on. You can continue to make good bets at small odds to the house and increase your chances of making a good score. You have to ask yourself if you're comfortable taking odds or laying odds. That is also an important consideration.

Come-Out Roll Percentages

Let's look at the possibilities of winning or losing immediately on the come-out. If you bet with the dice, there will be eight ways for you to win immediately, or 8 chances out of 36. This will happen theoretically 22.2% of the time. You'll lose immediately four times out of 36 rolls betting pass-line, or 11.1% of the time. The chances of a point number being rolled on the come-out will be 24 chances out of 36 possible combinations or 66.6% or 2/3 of the time.

When betting against the dice, the figures will be reversed as to immediate losses. You'll lose 22.2% of the time immediately, with the six ways the 7 can be made and the two ways the 11 can be rolled. You'll only win three out of 36 times or 8.3%, when the 2 (or 12) and 3 is rolled. One time out of 36, or 2.7% of the time, you'll have a push on the come-out roll.

Once you get past that come-out roll betting wrong, you're a favorite to win. There'll be three ways that either a 4 or 10 can be rolled. Since a 7 can be rolled six ways, the odds are 2-1 in your favor. There'll be four ways either a 5 or 9 can be rolled, making you a 3-2 favorite. There'll be five ways a 6 or 8 can be tossed giving you a 6-5 edge.

Free-Odds - Taking the Odds

If you look at a casino craps layout, nowhere will you see anything in printing saying free-odds. The casino doesn't advertise this option, but it is the single most important one you can have as a player. Here's how it works.

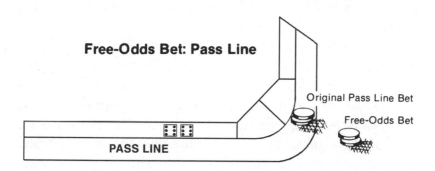

Free-Odds Bet: Pass Line

Original Pass Line Bet

Free-Odds Bet

PASS LINE

Once a point is established, the casino will permit you to make another bet in addition to your pass-line wager at the correct odds. In other words, on this free-odds wager, you will be paid off at 2-1 if the point is a 4 or 10. If the point is 5 or 9 you receive 3-2. With a 6 or 8, you'll get 6-5 if the point is repeated before a 7 shows on the dice.

Some casinos limit the free-odds bet to the amount you've bet on the pass-line. Thus, if you have $20 on the pass-line, you can only make up to a $20 free-odds wager. This is called **single odds**.

Many casinos will allow you to make a **double-odds bet**, that is, double your pass-line wager as a free-odds bet. Thus, if you've bet $20 on the pass-line, you can bet $40 as a free-odds bet.

If you never make a free-odds bet after making a pass-line wager, overall the house will have a 1.41% edge on your bet. If you make a single-odds wager after a free-odds bet, the house edge is now 0.8%. A double odds wager drops the casino advantage to 0.6%.

So, you see, it always pays to make the free-odds bet to the maximum allowed by the casino. Some casinos will allow you to wager 10 times the pass-line wager as a free odds bet. The house edge has now been reduced way down, where the game is practically an even one between you and the casino.

Let's assume you had the $20 bet on the pass-line and the come-out roll is a 9. You're playing in a casino that allows double odds bets. You now place $40 on the free-odds wager in addition to your original $20 pass-line bet. You place the chips behind the original chips, in the area separated by the bottom line of the pass-line space. Now, the dealer knows automatically that this is a free-odds wager.

Unlike the pass-line bet, which, once a point is established, cannot be removed by the player, a free-odds wager can always be taken down by the player at his option.

But a gambler shouldn't do this, for the free-odds bet is the only one where the house pays the correct odds and has no advantage whatsoever on a wager. Therefore, it is always to the player's advantage to make this bet.

Let's assume that the 9 is repeated before a 7 is thrown. What is the payoff? First, the player will receive $20 at even-money for his pass-line bet. Then for his $40 free-odds wager, he'll receive $60 at the correct 3-2 odds, for a total payout of $80.

What if a 7 is thrown before the 9 is repeated? Then the player will lose both his pass-line and free-odds wager. Although the player puts more money at risk by making a free-odds bet, he collects more if he wins, and most importantly, he reduces the edge the house has over his wagers. For that reason, when making a pass-line wager, make the maximum free-odds bet allowed by the casino.

When betting the pass-line and taking free-odds, all that will matter to you is whether the number is repeated or a 7 shows. All other numbers are immaterial to the winning or losing of the wager.

Free-Odds Bet - Examples

For example, suppose that the come-out roll is a 10. You've made a pass-line bet and now take the maximum free-odds bet. The shooter now throws an 11, 12, 2, 4, 5, 6, 8 and 9. None of these numbers affect you. Since it is not a come-out roll, the 11 doesn't make your bet a winner, and the 12 and 2 doesn't make it a loser. Now the roll continues - 3, 5 and 10. Since the 10 repeated before the 7 showed on the dice, you win both your pass-line and free-odds bets.

Let's follow another sequence. You make a pass-line wager and the point is an 8. You now make the maximum free-odds bet and wait to see what happens. The dice come up 4, 5, 5, 5, 9, 10, 3 and 7. You lose your pass-line and free-odds wagers because a 7 showed before an 8 was repeated. All the other numbers, including the run of three 5s, are immaterial to your wager.

So remember, a pass-line bettor may make a free-odds bet in addition to his or her pass-line bet. A single free-odds bet reduces the house edge from 1.41% to 0.8%, and it is further reduced to 0.6% for a double-odds bet. Maximum free odds bets should always be made by the player.

The house has no advantage on free-odds bets and pays the correct odds if the player wins. Although free-odds bets can be removed or reduced at any time, they should not be touched.

Needless to say, it pays to play craps in casinos that offer the most in free-odds wagers. If you have a choice of playing in a casino that offers single-odds or double-odds, by all means play where double-odds are allowed.

Laying Odds

When you're betting against the dice and there's a point number, you lay the correct odds against the number when you make a free odds wager. Note that we say you *lay odds*, rather than take them. Since any number rolled as a point number is at a disadvantage to a 7 being rolled, the odds are always against any number repeating before a 7 shows on the dice. For example, if a 4 or 10 is rolled, the odds are 2-1 against that number repeating before a 7 shows. A 5 or 9 is 3-2 against, a 6 or 8 is 6-5 against.

Suppose you had bet $10 on the don't pass line, and the point is a 4. Since the odds are 2-1 against that number repeating before a 7 comes up, if you lay single odds, you'd have to put down $20 behind the line as a free odds wager. You bet $20 because you're laying $20 to $10. Let's suppose that the shooter sevens out and you win your bet. You'd collect $10 on the don't pass wager at even-money, and an additional $10 on the free odds bet at 1-2.

When betting pass-line you take odds, while don't pass forces you to lay odds. Although both give the house the same edge, many players are reluctant to put out more money on the table than they'll be getting back, and that's one of the reasons the don't pass wager is not as popular as the pass-line bet.

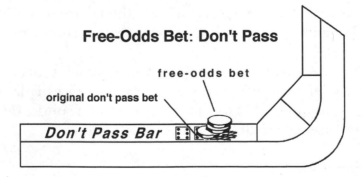

Free-Odds Bet: Don't Pass

free-odds bet

original don't pass bet

Don't Pass Bar

What happens if the shooter, instead of sevening out in the previous example, makes the 4? Then you lose both the $10 as your don't pass wager and the $20 free-odds bet.

You can always remove your don't pass wager, but that's inadvisable. The minute a point number is established, the odds are in your favor as a don't pass bettor. There are six ways to make a 7 and each of the point numbers can be made in fewer ways. If, by betting pass-line you're taking odds and getting bigger payoffs, why make don't pass wagers? As you gain experience in the game of casino craps, you'll be at tables where the dice are ice cold; where no points are ever repeated or made. When that happens, the don't or wrong bettors make a small fortune, as the dice move around the table with no shooter able to hold them for more than one series of rolls.

Players are under the impression that when you bet wrong, you're betting with the house. This is not the case. The casino will book all wagers whether pass or don't pass. But most of the bets will be with the dice, so the casino's interest is in having cold dice.

$10,000 Don't Pass Bet

But there are times when the casino bosses will pray for dice that pass, or win. I was at a table in a downtown Vegas casino where most of the players were betting in the $5-$25 range, when a high roller came and put down $10,000 in cash on don't pass. Suddenly the whole complexion of the game changed. The pit boss came over to watch the action.

The first shooter rolled a 9, then after rolling two other numbers, rolled a 7. The don't bettor now had $20,000. He said "let it ride." $10,000 in $500 chips were piled on top of the original cash bet. The dice moved to a small lady in her seventies. She shook the dice and rolled a 3. The

$20,000 had now expanded to $40,000. He let it ride once more. The lady now rolled a 4. The casino bosses sighed in desperation. A floorman was already calling upstairs, perhaps to have one of the owners show up to watch the action.

I had stopped betting to watch the little drama unfolding at the table. I looked over to the bettor. He was a man in his forties, with a lined angular face, and dark hair brushed straight back. He wore a Western shirt, with white studs running down the front. His hands were long, and I could see that his fingernails were buffed and clean. He waited patiently as the little old lady shook the dice. The buck was on the 4. He had 2-1 odds in his favor now. There were only three ways to make the 4 and the big 7 could come up six different ways.

The next roll was an 8. then a 5. I could see the pitboss wince as the first die showed an ace and the second spun off the 3 to the 4. The next roll was a deuce. The numbers were staying low. Then the shooter rolled a 7.

"Seven out, line away," said the stickman without much enthusiasm. The don't bettor had now won again. He had eighty thousand dollars piled up on the layout.

With both hands, the wrong bettor gathered up the chips and stacked them in the rails in front of him. He asked for a rack, and one materialized immediately in the pit. He stuffed the chips from the rails to the **rack**, a plastic container which holds chips, twenty to a row. There were four rows in the rack, so he was stuffing $500 chips, $10,000 to a row. He asked for another rack. Now he had $70,000 in chips stuffed in the two racks. The $10,000 in cash was still on the table. He picked it up and riffled the bills in his hands, and counted off five of them.

Dropping them on the table, he pushed them towards his dealer, and simply said, "for the boys." Then he stuffed the rest of the cash into his pockets and left the table. The casino was $70,000 poorer and the crew of dealers $500 richer.

In that case, the wrong bettor dominated the game, and he was the center of attraction. Often, at tables, everyone but one player will be betting with the dice, and the wrong better will merely get dirty looks from the others, because they know he's praying for the dice to lose while they're betting that the dice win. Never become upset by the attitude of other gamblers.

If you feel the dice are going to be cold, then bet against them. Go with your instincts if you find that they serve you well.

The Barred 2 or 12

One final note. If you study the layout, you'll notice that the 12 is barred on the don't pass line. In some casinos it's the 2 that is barred. It is immaterial which is barred, for each can be made in only one way, and represent 1/36 of the possible combinations of the dice or 2.7%. If neither number was barred as a winner on the come-out roll for the wrong bettors, then they'd have an advantage over the casino on a don't pass wager. In the private game of craps, neither number is barred as a craps number, and therefore, it always pays to bet against the dice on the come-out roll for that extra edge.

Should the barred number come out on the initial throw of the dice, then you neither win nor lose. It's simply a push. Your bet remains on the table. Expect this to happen theoretically once every 36 tosses of the dice on the come-out.

TAKING AND LAYING FREE-ODDS - FURTHER CONSIDERATIONS

Taking Odds - Special Bets

When betting with the dice on the pass-line, most of the time it will be easy to figure out just what you can bet as a free-odds wager. If you bet $10 on the pass line and are allowed to wager single odds, you simply bet another $10 behind the line. For double odds, you bet $20 as a free-odds bet.

However, if you bet an amount like $5 or $15 or $25, it becomes a little more tricky, especially if the point is a 5 or 9, which is paid off at 3-2. In that case, if the point is a 5 or 9, instead of betting $5 with a $5 pass-line wager, you'll be permitted to bet $6, so you can get the correct 3-2 payoff. Many casinos will not pay off with coins less than $1, so you don't want to bet $5 behind the line on a 5, and only get $7 back ($6 for the $14 and an extra dollar for the fifth dollar you bet.)

With the same numbers, if you wager $15 on the pass-line you'll be able to bet $20 behind the line, at $30-$20. The rule is simple - when betting three units, such as $15, you can bet four units, or $20 if the point is a 5 or 9. If you've bet $25 on the pass-line, then you can bet $30 behind the line on the 5 and 9.

When betting on the 4 or 10 as a point number, there's no problem. You simply bet an equal amount behind the line as single odds. If you've bet $15 on the pass-line you can only bet $15 behind the line, for a payoff of 2-1.

With a 6 or 8, we have a different situation. The payoff is 6-5, but most casinos will permit you to wager five units behind the line if you have three units on the pass-line. For example, suppose you've bet $15 on the pass line and the point is 8. Even though an additional $15 can easily be paid off by $18, the casino will allow you to bet $25 behind the line, for a payout of $30 if you win the bet.

Taking Advantage of Odds Bets

Since the more you can bet behind the line as a free-odds bet, the smaller the edge that casino has over you, it always pays to make the biggest possible odds wager. When you're playing in a casino that only allows single odds bets, make three-unit wagers on the line, so you can make a four unit wager if the point is 5 or 9, and a five-unit wager if the point is 6 or 8, behind the line. Take what the casino gives you for that little extra edge.

Most of the Nevada casinos will allow you to take at least double odds (some offer even more as an inducement to play in their casinos). The Lake Tahoe casinos, however, usually permit only single odds. In Atlantic City, single odds are the rule. So, when faced with single odds, in order to squeeze those extra free odds bets in, work out a method of only betting three units at a time on the pass-line.

When permitted to bet double odds take them! They reduce the house edge to 0.6%, and give you the chance to win the most money in the quickest time, for you're not getting paid off at even-money on free odds wagers, but you're getting the whole nine yards! You're getting the correct odds.

Let's assume that you encounter a shooter that is hot. Suppose you bet $25 on the pass-line and bet $50 behind the line, and the point is 4. He makes the point, and you collect $125 ($25 on the line bet and $100 for the free odds wager). Let's assume you leave $50 on the pass-line, and win that bet after the shooter's point is 9. You get $200 more as a payout ($50 on the line and $150 at 3-2 on the 9).

We'll assume that a 4 is the next point and you've put $75 on the linc and bct $150 behind the line. If you win that bet you collect another $375 ($75 for the line wager and $300 on the free odds bet at 2-1.) With three points being made, you've made a profit of $700 in a few minutes.

While you've been doing this, other players won't even make free-odds wagers, either out of ignorance or superstition. If they made the same line bets you did, their profit for the same three rolls would have been only $150. Not only did they miss the chance for a big win, but they allowed the house to hold a 1.41% edge over them instead of your 0.6%.

When the dice get hot, and smart craps players are making those double odds bets, the casino is in trouble, for it's going to take a big hit in its profits, and may even end up with a loss for the month. This has happened to a Las Vegas casino that recently went out of business. They took such a beating at the craps table one night that they changed their craps rules and wouldn't permit double odds anymore. So, be smart, and sock in those free-odds bets. They're your road to riches!

Come and Don't Come Bets

Many players are baffled by the Come and Don't Come bets and avoid them because they don't know how the wagers work. But they're fairly simple to understand, and we'll show you how to make them, and how they're paid off. A player should always keep these bets in his or her repertoire of wagers, for they offer great rewards while giving the house a minimum advantage.

Come Bets

If you recall, making a pass-line wager means that you are betting *with the dice*, for the dice to win. You want to see a 7 or 11 on that come-out roll, and if a point is established you want that point to be repeated before a 7 is rolled. In other words, you want the dice to pass. That's why the bet is called a pass-line wager.

The Come bet caters to your interest in having the dice win. What the Come bet allows you to do is make a series of additional wagers, all on the dice passing, after the come-out roll. Let's now see how this works.

Suppose the first roll of the dice, the come-out, is a 9. The buck is moved to the space 9 on the layout, and if you had bet a pass-line wager, you can now make a free-odds wager in addition to that bet. Let's assume that you've bet $10 on the pass-line. You're in a casino that allows double free-odds, so now you make an additional bet behind the pass-line as a free odds bet. You bet $20 here, at correct odds of 3-2. Now you have $30 working, $10 on the pass-line and $20 as a free-odds bet at 3-2.

Before the next roll of the dice, you can make an additional wager on the dice passing, by putting chips into the Come box. The next roll of the dice will win or lose for you exactly as the come-out roll did. *The only difference will be timing.*

Let's assume you put $10 into the Come box. If a 7 or 11 is thrown, you win that Come bet immediately. If a 2, 3 or 12 - craps - is thrown, you lose that bet immediately. Any other number, 4, 5, 6, 8, 9 or 10 becomes your Come point number, and it must be repeated before a 7 is rolled for you to win. If the 7 shows before the Come number is repeated, you lose that Come bet.

Free Odds on the Come

You can also take odds in the same way you took them on the pass-line. Let's assume the next roll is an 8. Since you're allowed double free-odds, you can make an additional $20 bet on the 8 repeating. You give the chips to the dealer and instruct him by saying simply "odds." He'll place the $20 in chips on top of the $10 in chips at a slight angle, to indicate an odds wager. And he'll place the chips in the center of the 8 place box.

Dealer will place free-odds bet atop original bet but offset to distinguish from come or don't come bet.

don't come and free-odds bet

come and free-odds bet

Now you have two numbers working for you, the 9, as the pass-line point, and the 8 as Come point. You can keep making Come bets until the shooter sevens-out, or until there's a new come-out roll. Let's see how this works later. But for now, we'll just follow the dice after a pass-line wager and one Come bet.

Sample Pass and Come Sequence with Free Odds

Let's assume the next number rolled is a 4. It is immaterial to your bets. All you're now interested in is the 9, the 8, and the 7. The 7 is a number you don't want to see.

The next number thrown is an 11. Also immaterial to you. Then the shooter rolls an 8. Since the 8 was a Come bet number you bet on, you've gotten yourself a winner.

Now that you've won, the dealer will remove the chips

from the 8 box and place them on the table near you, with additional winning chips. You get $10 profit for the original Come bet, and an additional $24 (on the $20 odds bet) at the correct 6-5 payoff.

At this moment, you only have the pass-line bet working. Let's assume you now make another Come bet, by placing $10 in the Come box. The shooter rolls 7. The 7 is a loser for your pass-line wager, and the $30 you bet on the pass-line and free-odds is taken away by the dealer. That's because a 7 showed before the 9 repeated as a point number.

However, since the 7 was the first roll for your Come bet, in essence a come-out for the Come wager, you win $10 for your Come bet.

Since the shooter sevened-out, there is a new come-out roll with another shooter. You can no longer make a Come bet till a point is established. All you can do now is make a pass-line wager.

So you see that the Come bet is identical in payouts and losses to the pass-line wager. The only difference is in the timing. The pass-line bet can only be made prior to the come-out roll, while the Come wager can only be made after the come-out roll.

The free odds bets are identical to the ones you can make on the pass-line. With Come bets, if you're allowed single odds, you can bet four units as an odds bet if the point is 5 or 9 and you've bet three units as a Come bet. If the point is 6 or 8, and you've bet three units as a Come wager, you can bet five units as a free-odds bets.

With double odds, you can bet double your Come bet as a free-odds bet on any Come number.

Sample Sequence #2

Let's follow another sequence. This time we'll make continuous Come bets. A new shooter is coming out, and we place $10 on the pass-line. He rolls a 4, and that's the point. We place $20 behind the line as our free-odds wager at 2-1, while the buck is moved to the 4.

We now place $10 into the Come box (two $5 chips.) The shooter rolls a 5. The chips are moved by the dealer to the center of the 5 box, and we give him an additional $20 in chips and say "odds." These chips are placed on top of the $10 in chips at a slight tilt, to designate that they're odds bets, not Come bets. Now we have the 4 and 5 working for us as a pass-line and Come bet.

We place another $10 in the Come box. An 11 is rolled. We win immediately and are paid $10 for our latest Come bet. We take away the $10 in winnings and leave our $10 in the Come box. A 3 is rolled. That's an immediately loser for us, and the dealer takes away our $10. Easy come, easy go. We put in another $10 in the Come box and the shooter throws an 8. The dealer takes the $10 and puts it into the 8 box, and we hand him $20 in chips and say "odds," and watch as the $20 is placed on the original chips in the 8 box.

Now we have three numbers working; the 4, 5 and 8. We place $10 more in the Come box, and the shooter rolls a 5. A winner! First, the dealer pays us off for the 5 by giving us $10 for our original come wager and an additional $30 ($30-$20) for our free-odds bet, for a total of $40.

That's all he has to do. The $10 can still stay in the Come box for the next roll. It's simply as they say, "off and on." What he could have done to make the situation more complicated is this - pay us $40, take the $10 bet from the Come bet and put it in the Come box, wait for us to give him $20 in odds and place another $10 in the Come box. But simply giving us $40 and leaving the $10 in the Come box and the $10 plus the $20 odds bet in the 5 box accomplishes the same thing.

Practice this at home, so you can see how it works. After we've been paid $40 for our winning 5 Come number, we still have three numbers working - the 4, 5 and 8. We re-established the 5 by having a Come bet on the last roll of the dice. If we didn't have a Come bet out, we'd have gotten $40 and the Come bet and odds bet would have been removed from the 5 number. But since we had a Come bet, we still have the three numbers working for us. And we have a Come bet out.

Let's assume the next roll of the dice is a 4, winning our pass-line wager. First of all our Come bet is moved to the 4 box, and we give the dealer an additional $20 as a free-odds wager. Then we collect $50 for our winning pass-line bet, $10 for the pass-line and $40 at 2-1 on our $20 free odds wager.

Now there's a new come-out roll, since the point was made on the pass-line. We place $10 in the pass-line box and can't make a Come wager until after the come-out. Let's assume the same shooter now rolls a 7. Here's what happens. We win $10 on our pass-line wager, but lose all three of our Come bets. However, since it's a come-out roll, *only the underlying Come bets are working, not the free odds bets on the Come numbers.* Thus $60 in free odds bets are returned to us, but we lose $30 for the three $10 Come bets.

Let's see how we stood on the last series of rolls.

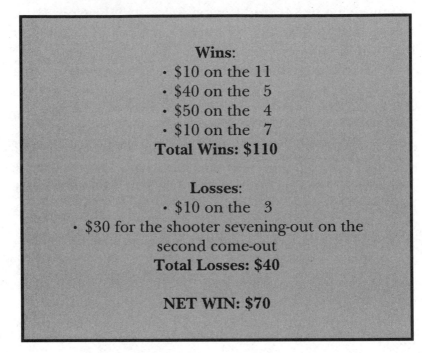

Wins:
- $10 on the 11
- $40 on the 5
- $50 on the 4
- $10 on the 7

Total Wins: $110

Losses:
- $10 on the 3
- $30 for the shooter sevening-out on the second come-out

Total Losses: $40

NET WIN: $70

Let's look at another series of bets to make sure we fully understand just how the Come bets work.

Free-Odds Sequence #3

We place $10 in the pass-line box, and the come-out roll is a 9. That's the point. We bet an additional $20 behind the line as a free-odds bet, and the buck is moved to the 9. Now we make our first Come bet of $10.

The shooter rolls a 5. This is our Come point, and our chips are moved by the dealer to the 5 box, and we give him an additional $20 as a free-odds bet at 3-2. The next roll, after we make another Come bet of $10, is an 8. Our Come bet is moved to the 8 box, and we give the dealer an additional $20 as a free-odds wager.

At this point, we decide we have enough bets out with three numbers working for us, the 9 as a pass-line point, and the 5 and 8 as Come points, all with double free-odds bets.

We have the right to make as many Come bets or as few as we want. Just because we made one Come bet doesn't mean we're obligated to make more. It's all at our option.

The next roll of the dice is a 9, winning our pass-line wager. We're paid off with $10 for the pass-line bet and $30 more at 3-2 for the free-odds wager for a total of $40.

There's a new come-out roll with the same shooter holding the dice. We make another pass-line wager of $10. The shooter rolls an 8, which is the new pass-line point. However, we have the 8 as a Come point. Since it's a come-out roll, the odds bets on the Come wagers aren't working, only the underlying bets. So our 8 Come bet is removed, and we're given back the $30 we bet ($10 on the Come bet and $20 on the free-odds) together with a payoff of $10 for our original Come bet.

At this moment, we have the following situation. We've already collected $50 in winnings; $40 for the pass-line win, and $10 for the 8 repeating on the come-out roll. We have two numbers working; the 8 as a pass-line wager and the 5 as a Come bet, both with maximum double free-odds. Now we put an additional $10 in the Come box.

The shooter rolls a 7. This 7 loses for our pass-line wager and our previous Come bet, for the 7 showed before either number had a chance to repeat. So we lose $60. But we've won our last Come bet of $10, since a 7 is an immediate winner for a Come wager.

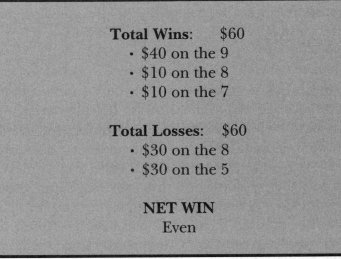

Total Wins: $60
- $40 on the 9
- $10 on the 8
- $10 on the 7

Total Losses: $60
- $30 on the 8
- $30 on the 5

NET WIN
Even

Come Bet Reminders

Remember the following:

• A Come bet can only be made after the come-out roll.

• You can make as many or as few Come bets as you wish, for any amount you care to, up to the house limit.

• You can make a Come bet, then wait several rolls to make another Come bet if you wish.

• Come bets are always working, even on the come-out roll. That is, they are subject to win or loss, but the free-odds bets are off on the come-out, but working otherwise.

• You can make the same free-odds wagers on the Come bets as you are allowed to make on the pass-line wagers.

• You can remove the free-odds wagers from your Come bets at any time, but this is not advised.

• You cannot remove your Come bet once it has been established as a Come point.

Remember those rules and you'll see how easy it is to follow the Come bets. Practice at home by making a makeshift layout showing a Come area and the boxes for the numbers 4, 5, 6, 8, 9 and 10 and throw the dice as if you're a shooter. Then make the bets with chips and pay yourself off or collect on losing bets. After fifteen minutes you'll get the feel of the game.

Come bets are very valuable. In our Winning Strategies section, we'll show you how to use them in an organized method to make the most of your potential profits. Come bets with free odds, like the pass-line wagers with free odds, reduces the house edge to it's minimum.

Don't Come Bets

Like Come bets, Don't Come wagers can only be made after the come-out roll. Don't Come bets serve the same purpose as don't pass wagers; they are used by the player betting against the dice, trying to make as many bets as possible that the dice will lose.

Don't Come bets can be enhanced with free-odds wagers. If the casino allows single odds, then the player lays the odds. For example, if a player has bet $10 on Don't Come and the Don't Come point is a 4, he lays $20 as a free-odds bet. That is a single odds wager, because the $20 is laid against $10. If double odds are allowed, then he lays $40 to $20.

The same holds true for other numbers. With the 5 or 9, if he has bet $10, then he lays $15 ($15-$10) as a single odds bet, and $30 ($30-$20) as a double odds bet. If the point is a 6 or 8, and he has bet $10 on the Don't Come, then he bets $12 ($12-$10) as a single odds wager, and $24 ($24-$20) as a double-odds bet.

If in doubt about what you can lay as a free-odds wager

after a Don't Come bet, ask your dealer for the maximum allowed. He'll gladly help you out. In the course of the game, anyone can get mixed up. So, let's say you've bet $15 on the Don't Come, and the next roll was a 6. Simply ask the dealer what you can bet. If it's single-odds he may say "$18" ($18-$15) or he may permit you to make a bigger odds bet. The bigger the better, for it lowers the house edge.

Even if you haven't made a Don't Pass bet, you're permitted to make a Don't Come wager. The same holds true for right bettors. you don't have to make a pass-line wager in order to make a Come bet.

Let's follow a typical roll of the dice to fully understand the Don't Come wagers.

Sample Don't Come Sequence #1

A new shooter is ready to roll the dice. We bet $10 on the don't pass line, in a casino where double odds are permitted. The first roll is a 3. We win $10. We pick up the winnings and keep our $10 bet going for the next come-out toss. It's a 4. The buck is moved to the 4 box, and we now make a free-odds bet, laying double odds next to our original bet. To do this, we have to put down $40 ($40-$20). We now put $10 in the Don't Come box. The next roll is a 7.

We lose the $10 we bet on the Don't Come, but we win $30 for our Don't Pass wager ($10 on the Don't Pass and $20 more for the free-odds bet we laid.)

Sample Don't Come Sequence #2

Now there's a new shooter, and a new come-out roll, for the previous shooter lost the dice when he sevened-out. We again place $10 in the Don't Pass box. The 7 is thrown and we lose our $10. We place another $10 in the box, for the new come-out roll.

It's a 5. We place an additional $30 ($30-$20) as a free-odds bet, by putting the odds bet next to the original wager. We now place $10 in the Don't Come box. The next throw is an 8. We hand the dealer $24 as a double free-odds bet on the 8 ($24-$20) and he moves our chips to the 8 box, and places it in the small area on top of the box, to differentiate this bet from those on the Come, which are placed below it in the middle of the 8 box.

Now we place another $10 in the Don't Come box. The next roll is a 6. We give the dealer another $24 for a double free-odds bet. Now we have bet against the following numbers. The 5 is our don't pass number, while we have the 8 and 6 as Don't Come numbers.

We decide not make any more Don't Come wagers, content with our three bets. The next roll is a 5. It's a loser for us as the 5 was the pass-line point, and we had bet Don't Pass. We lose $40 ($10 on the Don't Pass and $30 as our odds wager).

Now there's a new come-out roll by the same shooter. We place $10 in the Don't Pass box. He shoots a 7. We lose the $10, but win both our Don't Come bets, since a 7 showed on the dice before either the 8 or 6 was repeated.

On Don't Come bets, the bets and the odds on them are always working, in contrast to the Come bets, where only the underlying bets are working on the come-out. So we collect $30 for the 8 and $30 more for the 6.

We have no numbers working, as a new come-out roll by the same shooter is about to begin. It's the same shooter because he hasn't sevened-out yet. Let's see how we did on that series of rolls.

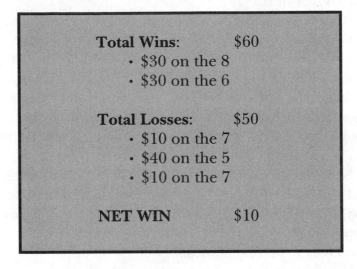

Total Wins: $60
• $30 on the 8
• $30 on the 6

Total Losses: $50
• $10 on the 7
• $40 on the 5
• $10 on the 7

NET WIN $10

Let's do one more series, to be absolutely sure we follow and understand the concept of Don't Come bets.

Sample Don't Come Sequence #3

We start with a $10 bet on the Don't Pass prior to the come-out roll. The toss is a 10, and that's the point. We now make a $40 wager at 2-1 as a free-odds bet next to the original wager. We put $10 into the Don't Come box, and the next throw is a 6. We give the dealer $24 as a double free-odds bet, laying 24-20 against the 6 repeating. We make another $10 wager on the Don't Come, and the next toss is a 5. We give the dealer an additional $30 as a 3-2 double odds bet against the 5 repeating. Again we bet $10 on the Don't Come, and the next throw is an 8. We give the dealer $24 (24-20) against the 8 repeating.

At this time, we now look over the layout to see what we've done. We have the 10 working as a Don't Pass wager. We have the 6, 5 and 8 as Don't Come wagers. All of these points are further bet against with double free-odds.

We make another $10 bet in the Don't Come box and the shooter rolls a 6. We thus lose our Don't Come wager on the previous 6, and lose $34. Our $10 is placed in the 6 box, and we give the dealer an additional $24 as a double free-odds bet. So we still have the same numbers working.

We make another $10 bet in the Don't Come box, and the shooter rolls a 7 and thus sevens-out. We lose the $10 wager, but win all our other bets.

Total Wins:	$120
• $30 on the 10	
• $30 on the 6	
• $30 on the 5	
• $30 on the 8	
Total Losses:	$44
• $34 on the 6	
• $10 on the 7	
NET PROFIT	$76

The wrong bettor who makes continuous Don't Come bets needs the 7 to show before several of the numbers get repeated for him to win. The kind of roll that just occurred is very favorable for him, since only one number, the 6 repeated before the 7 showed.

And he was able to make a number of Don't Come bets in the meantime, all of which won money for the gambler when the 7 came up on the dice.

Don't Come Bet Reminders

• A Don't Come bet can be made at any time after the come-out roll.

• You don't have to make a don't pass bet first in order to make a Don't Come bet.

• You can make as many Don't Come bets as you wish, for different amounts.

• You can make as few Don't Come bets as you wish.

• You don't have to make the Don't Come bets in consecutive order. You can wait for a roll or several rolls without making the bet.

• Anytime a number is repeated and you've established it as a Don't Come bet, you lose that bet.

• Although a 7 loses for you on the Don't Come, it enables you to win on all your established Don't Come and Don't pass wagers.

• Always bet the maximum odds as a free odds wager when playing in a double odds casino. The same holds true for a single odds casino. Play craps in a house that permits double odds rather than single odds if that situation is available in the jurisdiction you're playing in.

• When in doubt about how much you can wager as a free-odds bet, ask the dealer. He'll tell you the maximum limits available.

• You're always laying odds as a don't better; therefore you'll be collecting less than you put on the table.

• When betting against the dice, Don't Come bets are very valuable as a tool for making money for you. They allow you to collect on several bets when the dealer sevens-out, and reduce the house edge to the minimum.

7. THE OTHER BETS

Place Number Bets

		PLACE	BETS		
4	5	SIX	8	NINE	10

The place numbers are the same as the points in craps. They are the 4, 5, 6, 8, 9 and 10. The casino allows the player to bet on these numbers so that, if they repeat before a 7 is thrown, the player will be paid at better than even-money odds.

Place Numbers Odds and Payoffs

First, let's see what the odds are on the various number. The 4 and 10 will be paid off at 9-5. The 5 and 9 will get a payout of 7-5, and the 6 and 8 will receive 7-6 as their payouts.

We already know that the correct payoffs for each number is higher. The 4 and 10 should be paid off at 2-1, for there are only three ways to make a 4 or 10 and six ways to make a 7. By only paying off at 9-5, the house makes a profit of 6.67% on this wager.

The 5 and 9 can each be made four ways, while the 7 can be rolled six ways. Therefore the odds against repeating a 5 or 9 before a 7 is rolled is 3-2. By only paying off at 7-5, the house edge is 4.0% on this bet.

The 6 and 8 can each be made in five ways, while the 7 can be tossed six ways. The correct odds here are 6-5, while the casino pays 7-6, for an advantage on these wagers of 1.52%.

Knowing this, let's see how these bets are made.

How To Make Place Bets

Gamblers usually wait till the come-out roll has been thrown before betting on the place numbers, because these bets are off or not working on the come out. Bettors who wager on place numbers are betting that the dice will win, or pass. They want the point or place numbers to keep repeating and they don't want to see a 7. A 7 after a come-out not only loses all pass-line wagers and come bets, but also loses for all place numbers.

Patience Pays Dividends

At the craps table, the usual procedure for right bettors is to make a pass-line bet and then take odds, either single or double, or whatever the house permits. A pass-line wager with single odds gives the house only 0.8%, while at double odds, it is further reduced to 0.6%. These are smart bets.

As we showed in the previous sections, it would be wise to now make Come bets, for the house has the same low edge on these wagers. But many gamblers are impatient, and for their impatience they pay the price. In order to have a Come bet working for you, you have to establish it by first making a Come wager and then seeing a Come point number rolled. Then you have to make another Come wager and have a second Come point number established.

However, the impatient gamblers can't wait. They want to have all the numbers established at once, so that, if any are thrown, they get an immediate payout. Let's follow two players. **Player A** makes Come bets; **Player B** makes place bets.

Place Bets Compared #1

Player A, after making a pass-line wager and taking double free-odds, makes a Come bet. The shooter rolls a 6. That is a Come point, and the player now gives the dealer double-odds to lay on the 6. Then he makes another Come wager and the shooter rolls an 8. Now he gives the dealer double-odds again, and has two numbers besides the pass-line point working from him. So far, he hasn't collected anything.

Player B, after making a pass-line wager and taking double free-odds, now covers all the remaining place numbers with chips. Let's assume the point on the come-out is 10. Wishing to bet at least $10 on each place number, he gives the dealer $54, and says "across the board." The dealer takes this phrase to mean "cover all the remaining place numbers." Since the 10 is the point, he leaves it alone, for the gambler already has a bet on that number on the pass-line.

The dealer places $10 on the 4, 5 and 9. He also places $12 on the 6 and $12 on the 8. Why does he do this in this way? Remember, the 4 is paid off at 9-5, so a $10 bet will net the player $18 if it's repeated. The 5 and 9 are each paid off at 7-5, so **Player B** can expect $14 if either the 5 or 9 repeats.

The 6 and 8 are paid off at 7-6, so each $12 bet will give the player $14 if one of those numbers is thrown before the 7 comes up.

Now, going back a bit, we recall that **Player A** was establishing two come points, the 6 and 8, and collected nothing while this was going on.

But **Player B** collects $14 for the 6 and another $14 for the 8. He already has $28 back in his rails. And any other point or place number that comes up will give him more of a payout.

Why isn't this a good thing them? First of all, none of the bets he is making on place numbers gives the house less than a 1.52% edge. The worst is the 4 at 6.67%, while the Come bettor backed by double odds never gives more than 0.6% as his house edge.

Also, all the bets are at risk from the second roll on, the roll after the come-out roll. Let's see this in a horrible example, one that happens often at a craps table.

Place Bets Compared #2

Player A bets $10 on the pass-line and the point is 5. He puts $20 behind the line as a double free-odds bet, and makes a Come bet of $10. The shooter, holding cold dice, immediately sevens-out. The loss for **Player A** is $20. He wins $10 on the Come bet because of the 7, but loses $30 for his pass-line wagers, for a net loss of $20.

Now let's look at **Player B's** situation. He bets $10 on the pass-line and $20 behind the line on the 5 as a point. Now he gives $54 to the dealer to spread on all the place numbers. The shooter rolls a 7. **Player B** has lost $84, $54 on his place numbers, all of which lose when a 7 is tossed, and $30 on his pass-line and free odds bets.

A few cold rolls like this, and **Player B** will not only be muttering to himself but might run out of money. Those $84 losses add up fast. **Player A** is going slower, and being patient. In the long run, he'll do much better than **Player B**. For one thing, he's not giving up the same edge that **Player B** is to the house.

Attractive Feature of Place Bets

There's one other big reason why many players bet on the place numbers. They remain working longer than Come numbers, especially if a 7 is rolled on the come-out. Let's explain with an example.

Player A bets $10 on the pass-line. The point is 8 and he makes an additional $20 bet behind the line. He now makes a Come bet of $10, and the Come point is 9. He again makes a $20 free-odds bet. The next roll is an 8. he wins $34 for his pass-line and free-odds bets. Now there's another come-out roll.

The same shooter throws a 7. Having made an additional $10 bet on the pass-line, **Player A** wins another $10. However, his come bets, established on the 9 and 8 are losers. He loses $20, while the free-odds bets are returned to him since they aren't working on the come-out. So he has to begin all over again in establishing Come point numbers after the come-out establishes a new point.

Player B makes the same pass-line bet and takes double odds. He now puts $52 on the place numbers. The first roll of a 9 nets him $14, and the 8 makes him a winner on the pass-line for another $34.

He makes a $10 bet on the pass-line and the shooter throws a 7. He wins his $10 pass-line wager, but his place bets aren't affected by the 7. *Place bets are off on the come-out roll*. Therefore, assuming the next number thrown on the dice is a 9, he still has all his place numbers intact.

He had originally bet $52 instead of $54, because the point had been an 8. Therefore, he had to put $10 each on the 4, 5, 9 and 10 and only $12 on the 6. Now, with the point being a 9, he directs the dealer to move his place bet on the 9 to the 8, and must give the dealer $2 more so that he's betting $12 on the place number 8. Now he has $54 on the place numbers.

Sometimes, in the course of a long and hot roll, a roll in which numbers are constantly repeated, no 7 comes up except on the come-out after a point has been made. When that happens, the Come bettor has to begin again, while the place bettor keeps racking in the money.

However, those old devil odds keep getting in the way, and the place bettor will get hurt in the long run, giving away from 1.52% to 6.67%.

The casino has set this rule about place numbers not working on the come-out, just to seduce players into making these bets, hoping for that big hot roll. But in the meantime they have set up prohibitive odds, and will eat up the players' bankrolls in the long run.

Should place bets ever be made?

Yes, but only on the 6 and 8, each of which can be made five ways. These two numbers will be at the heart of a hot roll, coming up most often, and the casino edge isn't that bad, at 1.52%. Some aggressive Come bettors will establish two or three numbers and then place the 6 and 8 or either one when they haven't yet been established by the pass-line or Come rolls. Only in that case are they worth-while. In our analysis of systems and methods, we'll examine this situation thoroughly.

Making the Most of Place Bets

We've shown, for illustrative purposes, a player making place bets so that each number is covered for $10, with the 6 and 8 covered for $12 each. This means, when all the numbers but the pass-line point are bet as place numbers, an expenditure of either $52 or $54. It's $52 if only one of the 6 or 8 numbers is a place number, and $54 if both are. What's the difference? To refresh your recollection, if the pass-line point is a 4, 5, 9 or 10, all called **outside numbers**, then $54 is necessary to cover the place numbers for at least $10, with $12 each on the 6 and 8. Should a 6 or 8 be the pass-line point number, then only $52 is necessary.

Though we used the $10 and $12 betting schemes as illustrations, gamblers are permitted to bet less. They can bet $5 on the 4, 5, 9 and 10, for payoffs of $9 for the 4 and 10, and $7 for the 5 and 9. They can bet a minimum of $6 on the 6 and 8 as well, for payoffs of $7 on these numbers.

If you bet less than $5 on the outside numbers (4, 5, 9 and 10) or less than $6 on the 6 or 8, you'll only be paid off at even-money, so never do this, for you give the casino a monstrous edge. For example, instead of 1.52% on the 6 and 8, the house advantage jumps to 9.09%. So remember, when making place bets, only bet in multiples of $5 on the outside numbers and in multiples of $6 on the 6 and 8. The one exception is the casino which will pay off a $3 place bet on the 6 or 8 with $3.50.

If in the heat of the game, you get a little mixed up, the dealer will be there to help you. Just ask him how much should be bet. For example, suppose you have $32 in chips and you want to cover the 6 and 8 as place numbers. He'll tell you that you can bet either $12 on each one for a total of $24, or a total of $36, if you want to put $18 on these numbers. You can either take change or give the dealer $4 extra. Don't be ashamed or embarrassed by asking questions. It's better than being a fool and getting paid even-money for part of that bet if the dice come up 6 or 8.

Removing, Raising and Lowering Place Bets

Place bets can be made at any time, but they are working, or operative, only after the come-out roll. They can be made in any amount subject to the maximum house limit, which might be as low as $500 or as high as $3000, or even higher.

There's no hard and fast rule that says you have to cover all the place numbers at once. You can cover only one, or as many as you want. You can cover different place numbers in different amounts. For example, you can put $60 each on the 6 and 8 and $5 on the 5, if that's what you wish to do. You can remove or **take down** place numbers at any time, or declare them **off**. They won't be working till you once more declare them *working*.

You can also add to or subtract from place numbers after every roll of the dice. Many gamblers, going for that one big score with a hot roll, press their bets constantly. By **press** we mean increase the bet. Here's how many of them do this.

Pressing Place Bets

Suppose a gambler has put down $54 across the board, covering all the place numbers. A 5 is rolled. Instead of taking the payout of $14 (14-10) he says "press it," to the dealer. The dealer will put $10 of the payout on the 5 and give the player $4. Now the player has $20 on the 5. Let's say the next number is a 6. He'll say "press it," again, and the dealer will put another $12 on the 6, and give the player $2.

What the gambler is reasoning is this - that these numbers are "hot" and will repeat again, and each time they repeat, up to a certain point, he'll increase the amount he has bet with the casino's money. Of course, his reasoning is fallacious. First of all, each throw of the dice is independent of any previous throw. The dice have no memory. Any number can show next. And he isn't increasing the bets with the casino's money - he's increasing the bets with his money. Each payout belongs to the player. He can either keep it in the rails in front of him or bet it. That's his choice.

The trouble with pressing bets in this way is that most of the profits end up as bets and after a hot roll, all the gambler has is pennies instead of a big score. Here's why. Let's go back to our gambler, who has already pressed the 5 up to $20 and the 6 to $24. Let's say the next roll is another 5. He says "press it," and now instead of getting $28 as a payout (28-20) he leaves $20 on the number and takes back $8. In essence, he's doubling the bet he has out there each time it repeats. If it keeps repeating, fine, but there will be a time when the 7 shows.

I've seen gamblers press their bets five and six times, and then a 7 shows, and all their payouts are pittances. If you're going after a hot roll and want to bet place numbers, in our section on systems and methods of betting, we'll show you how to do it sanely, so you can still take advantage of the hot roll, and still make a big score.

When covering all the numbers as place bets, you need at least four numbers to show to make a profit. Here's how we figure it.

Suppose you put out $52. You've covered the 4, 5, 6, 9 and 10. We'll assume that the numbers thrown will be in order of the place numbers. If a 4 is thrown, you get back

$18, then $14 for a 5 and $14 for a 6. That gives you a payout of $46. You're still $6 short and if a 7 is now thrown, you lose an aggregate of $6 on your place bets. Thus you need the fourth number thrown to give you that profit. If it's a 6, 5 or 9, you get back $14 more for a profit of $8.

Place Bet Summary

So now we understand that place numbers can be bet in various ways. They can be increased after each roll if the player desires. They can also be decreased or removed after any particular roll of the dice. Simply tell the dealer to remove them, and they'll all go back to you to insert in your rails.

However, some gamblers get hunches during the course of play. Let's assume a high roller has $540 out there, with $100 on the outside numbers and $120 each on the 6 and 8. Suddenly he feels a 7 coming up with the dice. But he doesn't want the hassle of having the bets removed and then reinstated. So he tells the dealer "off on the place numbers."

The dealer will put a little "off" tag on the numbers indicating that they're not working at all. Let's say that numbers keep repeating, and the gambler is sorry he said "off." Or he simply says "they're working again," and the "off" tag comes off, and the place numbers are once again subject to wins or losses.

Place numbers have all this leeway because the house wants you to play them. It gets a big advantage from the place bets, because at a crowded table with the dice moderately hot, they get a ton of action.

Buying the 4 and 10

Betting on the 4 and 10 gives the house the biggest edge of all the place numbers, 6.67%. To reduce this advantage, gamblers *buy* the 4 and 10 or either number. What they do is give the house an immediate commission of 5% and then are paid off at 2-1. Here's how this works.

In casinos where coins are used at the craps tables, a gambler can bet $10 on the 4 and give the dealer 50¢ at the same time. He tells the dealer he's *buying the 4*. The dealer will place a small "buy" button on the chips, so he'll know they're bought, and if the 4 repeats, instead of 9-5, the player will get back 2-1 as his payout.

In casinos where no coins are used, in order to buy the 4 or 10 the player will have to bet at least $20. He can buy the 4 and 10 for $10 each and give the dealer $1 as his 5% commission. That's ok. Now he'll get a 2-1 payout if either number repeats.

By doing this the house edge is reduced to 4.76%. I'm always amazed by many big gamblers who bet heavily on the 4 and 10 and don't have the sense to buy them and get not only better payouts but at the same time reduce the house edge by nearly 2%.

Like the place bets, buy bets can be removed, added to or reduced at any time after any roll of the dice.

Lay Bets

It is rare to see anyone **lay bets**, that is, bet against specific numbers. It's the equivalent of place numbers for the wrong bettors, but with one significant difference. A lay bettor must pay a 5% commission each time he makes a lay wager. Here's how this works.

Let's assume a player has made a don't pass wager and laid odds. He's made a couple of Don't Come bets as well.

But now he feels that a 7 is imminent, and he wants to take advantage of his hunch. So he bets against all the other numbers by laying bets. We'll assume that the don't pass point is a 6, while the two Don't Come point numbers are 8 and 9. The dice have been cold and no one has held them for any length of time in the last half-hour. So he lays bets against the remaining numbers, 4, 5 and 10.

To do this, he informs the dealer that he's *laying bets*. Let's assume he wants to bet $40 against the 4 and 10. Since the payoff at 1-2 if he wins is $20, he gives the dealer $2, representing 5% of $40 ($20 + $20) on the 4 and 10. Remember, it's not 5% of his wager, as it is in buying the 4 and 10. It's 5% of the *potential payout* if he wins his bet by the 7 showing on the dice. If he lays $30 on the 5, since the payoff will be $20, he gives the dealer another $1. Now he has all the numbers covered as a wrong bettor. If a 7 shows on the next roll of the dice, he's made a nice score. Of course, if any of the numbers he's bet against, including the lay bets, are repeated, he loses those bets and chips, and has to make additional lay bets if he wants to keep all the numbers covered.

The house edge on lay bets isn't that high, compared to place bets. Laying against the 4 or 10 is 2.44%, against the 5 or 9 is 3.23%, and against the 6 and 8 is 4%. Note that these figures are smaller on the outside numbers and higher on the 6 and 8, the exact opposite of place numbers.

Like place numbers, the lay bets can be removed, increased or decreased after any roll of the dice, at the player's discretion.

To differentiate lay wagers, a "buy" or "lay" button will be placed on the chips, and they'll be moved into that small area above the particular place number you're betting against.

Field Bets

The **Field Bet** takes up a large area of the craps layout, far larger in proportion to the action it gets in actual play. The Field Bet is used primarily by two types of gamblers. First, the novice, who sees all those numbers that will win for him or her, and knows also that there is a win or lose decision after each roll of the dice. Not understanding how to make the other, better wagers, the beginner makes Field Bets.

Secondly, the Field Bet is used by systems players. They know that the odds aren't as bad as roulette (though actually they are where both the 2 and 12 are paid off at 2-1) and they can work a system where each throw of the dice means a win or lose decision.

If they try their systems on the pass-line or don't pass bets, there is a long wait till the final result will be known. However, with a Field Bet, they win or lose right away, after each roll of the dice. Thus, they can start with $1 and double their bet after a loss or use whatever system they follow. In the long run, however, with the house edge close to 3% at best and 5.55% at the worst, its hard for any system to overcome those percentages and end up a winner.

Let's see how the Field Bet works. The player puts chips on his own into the Field Bet area, and if any of the numbers that are shown, the 2, 3, 4, 9, 10, 11 or 12 come up on the very next throw of the dice, he wins his bet. He gets paid even-money for all numbers except the 2 and 12, which are circled. In some casinos the 2 and 12 both pay 2-1; in others either the 2 or 12 pays 3-1 while the other number pays 2-1.

Suppose you put a $5 chip into the Field Bet area. The next throw of the dice is a 9. You win at even-money. If the throw was a 2 and it pays 3-1, you win $15. If the throw had been a 12 at 2-1, you'd win $10. However, if the throw had been any number other than those shown in the Field Bet area, you'd lose your bet.

The Field Bet looks like a good thing, with all those numbers working for the player, plus the enhanced 2-1 and 3-1 payout for the 2 and 12. But is it?

Let's examine the situation more closely. The 2 and 12 can be made one way each. That adds up to two ways. The 3 and 11 can be made two ways each. That now totals six ways. The 4 and 10 can each be made three ways; so our total is now twelve ways. And the 9 can be made four ways, for a grand total of sixteen ways to make all these numbers. But since the 2 and 12 in some casinos are paid off at 2-1, we add two more ways, for a total of 18.

Let's look at it on a chart. In this chart, we'll assume the 2 and 12 is paid at 2-1.

Winning Numbers - Field Bet	
Number	Ways to Make
2	2
3	2
4	3
9	4
10	3
11	2
12	2
Total	18

If either the 2 or 12 is paid off at 3-1, then there are nineteen ways to get paid off. Now let's examine the missing numbers and see how many ways they can be made.

Losing Numbers - Field Bet	
Number	Ways to Make
5	4
6	5
7	6
8	5
Total	20

We see that the four losing numbers contain twenty different ways to throw them. So, depending upon the casino we play at, the chances of making a Field Bet winning wager will either be 20-18, or 20-19 in the casino's favor.

If both the 2 and 12 are paid of at 2-1, and the odds are 20-18, then the house has a 5.55% edge in its favor. If the chances are 20-19, the house edge is 2.77%. We can immediately compare this advantage to a pass-line, Come, don't pass, Don't Come bet with free odds. With single odds the house edge would be 0.8%; with double free odds allowed, it would be 0.6% in the house's favor. Therefore, the Field Bet is not that good a wager. Even betting on the place numbers 6 and 8 is better, for the house edge on those place bets is only 1.52%.

Then why bet the Field? As we have shown, it is made by novices, and by systems players. The Field Bet is the first of the one-roll bets we've studied, where the outcome is determined by the very next roll of the dice. Our advice? Don't make this wager.

Big 6 and Big 8 Bets

Finally we come to the last of the bets that can be made by players on either side of the table. The areas which accommodate the Big 6 and Big 8 bets are rather big for wagers that get very little action. In fact, only completely ignorant novices ever make this bet.

When you bet on the Big 6 or Big 8, or both, you're betting that the 6 or 8, or both will come up before a 7 is thrown. We already know that a 6 can be made five ways, as can an 8. There are six ways however to make a 7. Therefore, the odds of a 7 coming up before a 6 is repeated is 6-5. The same holds true for the 8. But the bet is paid off at even-money, giving the house an enormous 9.09% advantage on this wager.

If a player feels that the 6 and 8 or either one will come up, he'd be much wiser to make a place bet on the 6 or 8. If he puts down a minimum of $6 in most casinos, he'll be paid off at 7-6, giving the house only a 1.52% edge on the wager. In some casinos, where smaller action is permitted, the house will permit $3 bets on the 6 and 8, paying them off at $3.50 to $3.00, the same 7-6 odds with the same house edge.

The only exception to making this wager is in the casinos in Atlantic City, where, for the convenience of gamblers, the houses permit bets on the Big 6 and Big 8 to be paid off the same as place bets, at 7-6. But in order to get this payoff, you must bet $6 or multiples of $6. For example, if you bet $10, you'll be paid $7 for the first $6, and then even-money on the next $4.

But if you're not in Atlantic City, or any casino where the payoff is not 7-6 on the Big 6 and Big 8, don't make this bet. There's no reason to make it, and the house edge will eat you up.

The Proposition Bets

The **proposition** or **center bets** are under the control of the stickman. If any player wants to make any of these wagers, he hands his chip or chips to the dealer, who delivers them to the stickman, usually by throwing them to him, and telling him what bet or bets to make.

The bets can be divided into two distinct sections. First there are the **one-roll wagers**, which are determined by the next throw of the dice. Then there are the other bets, known as **hardways**, which may take several rolls to determine their outcome.

All of the bets discussed in this chapter are bad bets for the player. The house edge runs high, and the first of the bets we'll discuss has the highest casino advantage of any single wager on the craps table.

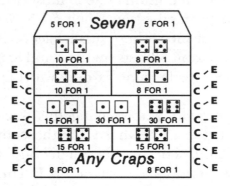

The One-Roll Wagers

Since the very next throw of the dice determines the outcome of these bets, they're always working, subject to an immediate win or loss.

Any Seven

By making this wager, the player is betting that the very next roll of the dice will come up 7. If any other number shows, it's a loser. The chances of rolling a 7 is 5-1, since there are 36 combinations on the dice, and only six ways to make a 7. However, the casino pays off at only 4-1, and gives itself a 16.67% advantage!

It's a sucker bet, and even the dumbest of craps players know to stay away from it. Then who makes the bet on the 7? I guess it's left to the brain deads, for I can't see any possible reason to make this wager.

Don't even think of making this bet.

Any Craps

When making this bet, the player is wagering that the next roll of the dice will either be a 2, 3 or 12. If any of these numbers comes up, the payoff will be 7-1. The chances of a craps showing on the dice at any time is 4 in 36, or 8-1. Therefore, the house exacts an advantage over the bettor of 11.1%. It's a huge edge. Why do gamblers make this bet? It's made mostly on the come-out by bettors who have a big pass-line wager and want to "protect" their bet. But at 11.1%, they're not protecting anything but the casino's profits. Never, under any circumstances, be tempted by this wager.

2 or 12

When making this wager, you're betting that the next throw of the dice will be a 2, if that's the number you're betting on, or the 12, if that's the number you've selected. There is only one way to make either number, and thirty-five ways to roll other numbers. Therefore, the correct odds are 35-1 against either number showing.

Casinos pay either 30-1 on this bet, giving them an edge of 13.89% (double digits again!), or, if the casino is really greedy, it only pays 30 *for* 1. This is a payoff of only 29-1, and gives the house an advantage of 16.67%, matching the worst bet on the layout.

There's no reason to make this bet, for it's strictly a sucker's wager.

3 or 11

The 3 can only be made in two ways, 2-1 or 1-2, and the 11 can be made in the same two ways, 6-5 and 5-6. The true odds against making either number is 17-1. But you can't get that payoff anywhere. The best you can hope for is 15-1, which gives the house an edge of 11.1%. In the greedier places, the payoff is only 15 for 1, or 14 to 1 (the same thing), giving the house an edge of 16.67%. Let the suckers and dead brains make this wager. Avoid it yourself.

The Horn Bet

Some casinos have a *horn bet*, which is an expanded any craps wager. In addition to the 2, 3 and 12, they throw in the 11 as well. When you bet the horn, you've got all four numbers covered, and if the next roll of the dice is a craps or an 11, you're a winner.

To make this bet, you have to bet in units of four chips. One for each number. The trouble here is that the payoff is at the usual bad casino edge. In other words, the casino will be taking between 11.1% and 16.67% depending upon which number comes up.

Thus, the casino is making it easy for you to make four bad bets at once, rather than grinding you out one at a time. Like any other bet on the center of the layout, avoid this wager.

The Hardway Bets

The hardways are not one-roll bets. It may take a while for these bets to win or lose. What the bets are in essence, is this - you're wagering that one of the point numbers you're betting on will come up hard before it comes up easy, or before a 7 is rolled.

What do we mean by *hard*, or *hardway?* Pairs are

hardways. 2-2 is the *hard* 4. 3-3 is the *hard* 6. 4-4 is the *hard* 8 and 5-5 is the *hard* 10. Other pairs on the dice can't be bet as hardways, since they're not point numbers.

To calculate the odds on hardways, we first note that a hardway can only be made in one way. It can be made more often as an *easy* number (that is, not as a pair) and of course, the good old 7 can be rolled six ways. Let's examine the hardways to determine the house edge.

Hard 4 and Hard 10

We can group the hard 4 and hard 10 together, for each of these numbers can be made in only three ways, and two of those ways are easy. Thus, a 4 can be rolled easy as 1-3 or 3-1, and the 10 can be rolled easy as a 4-6 and 6-4. We know the 7 can be rolled in six ways. Therefore, there's one way to roll a 4 or 10 as a hardway, and eight ways to roll either an easy way or a 7. Thus, the odds against rolling the hard 4 or the hard 10 before they come up easy or a 7 shows are 8-1.

The casino only pay 7-1 on either the hard 4 or the hard 10, giving it an advantage of 11.1% over the gambler.

Hard 6 and Hard 8

It's even harder to roll a hard 6 or hard 8, because there are more ways to make these numbers easy. The 6 can be rolled as an easy number in the following ways: 1-5, 5-1, 2-4 and 4-2.

That's four ways. The 7 can be rolled in six ways. That's ten ways to lose on this bet. There's only one way to roll a 6 hard. The odds against the hard 6 is therefore 10-1.

With the hard 8 we have the same situation. The 8 can be rolled easy as follows: 2-6, 6-2, 3-5 and 5-3. And the 7 can be rolled six ways. So again, we have a 10-1 situation.

The house only pays off at 9-1 however, giving it an advantage of 9.09%. This is better than the edge it has on the hard 4 and hard 10, but it's nothing to get excited about. It's just too much, and no astute player should ever bet on the hardways.

Who does make hardway bets? A lot of gamblers. They usually do this during a roll where numbers are being thrown and the dice are hot. They feel lucky and keep making hardway bets over and over. We mean that literally, for if the gambler is covering all the hardways, he may have to keep replenishing his wagers after every roll of the dice.

For example, he covers each of the hardways with $10 bets, putting out $40. The point is 9. The first roll after the come-out is a 6, made 4-2. Down goes $10 of the gambler's money. He throws out another $10 on the hard 6. The next roll is an 8 as 5-3. Down goes the hard 8, and still another $10 has to be thrown to the stickman if the player wants all the hardways covered. The next roll is another 8, made 6-2, and another $10 goes out.

The gambler may have all these numbers covered as place numbers for bigger sums, but in the end, he may find after a moderately hot roll that he has expended over $100 on the hardways, money he'd be better off keeping in his rails. I've seen more money wasted on hardways than on any other bets.

Other players make hardways bets as ways to toke a crew of dealers. They'll throw out a $5 chip and say, "hard 6 for the boys", when the point number is a 6. *The boys* know this is a bad bet and would rather have the $5 in their hands, but they take the tokes any way they can.

Still other gamblers want to urge the pass-line point to be made, and always bet it as a hardway if the point is a 4, 6, 8 or 10. More wasted money.

Hop Bets

The **hop bet** accommodates those gamblers who want to make a hardway bet into a one-roll wager. So they make a hop bet, betting that the next roll of the dice will come up as a pair. For example, they tell the dealer they're making a hop bet on the 4, that it'll come up as 2-2.

The odds against any particular pair coming up is always 35-1, since a pair can only come out in one way, while there are thirty-five ways it can lose. When a player makes a hop bet, he's only paid off at 30 for 1, in reality, 29-1. This gives the house an edge on this bet of 16.67%, the very highest it has on the layout.

Why would anyone make a hop bet? I really don't know. Most craps players don't even know such a bet exists, and in this case, ignorance is a good thing. Don't even think about hop bets. They're for suckers.

Most of the one-roll proposition bets in the center of the layout get heavy action before the come-out, with pass-line players "protecting" their bets by wagering on the Any Craps. They figure that if they bet $25 on the pass-line and an additional $5 on Any Craps, if a craps comes up, they get back $20 and only lose $5, instead of the full $25 for the pass-line loss. But this reasoning is seriously flawed. They're much better off losing the $25 occasionally (four times every 36 rolls) than constantly making a bet that gives the house an 11.1% edge. The craps will rarely come up. More often, the 7 or 11 will show. So the bettor loses $5 for his Any Craps bet while wining $25 on his pass-line wager. He's just punishing himself this way.

The casino encourages the proposition bets. Before the come-out, the stickman will be telling the players to get down on that *craps, eleven,* and his call is usually followed by a flurry of activity as chips are arranged up and down the center layout on the rounded "c" and "e" circles that stand for "Any Craps," and "11." They're all wasted bets. Though they may win sometimes, they're big losers in the long run, and eat away at any player's bankroll.

After the come-out, when the point is established, the call of the stickman is once more heard. He wants to encourage the players to make the hardway bets. If the pass-line point is an even-number, say, a 6, he'll cry out, *bet the hard six, bring it out.* By bring it out, he means have it show on the dice.

If the dice could hear what he's saying, it might be worthwhile. But unfortunately, those plastic rascals have no ears, and no eyes either. They just do their thing, impervious to all the yelling and praying going on at the craps table. It's all random chance.

When you're at the table, and the dice get hot, and everyone is betting those hardways, or protecting their pass-line wagers by betting on the Any Craps, don't get caught up in the foolishness. Even if everyone else at the table has the fever, doesn't mean you have to make stupid bets. Stay above the fray. In the long run it'll help your bankroll. It'll be the difference often times between leaving the table a winner or a loser.

The following chart will show you all the bets that can be made on the layout, and the odds on each and every one of the bets. Study them and remember the best bets.

COMPLETE ODDS ON ALL THE BETS

BET	PAYOUT	CASINO EDGE
Line Bets		
Pass-Line	Even-money	1.41%
with Single Odds	Even-money plus odds	0.8%
With Double Odds	Even-money plus odds	0.6%
Come	Even-money	1.41%
With Single Odds	Even-moncy plus odds	0.8%
With Double Odds	Even-money plus odds	0.6%
Don't Pass	Even-money	1.40%
With Single Odds	Even-money plus odds	0.8%
With Double Odds	Even-money plus odds	0.6%
Don't Come	Even-money	1.40%
With Single Odds	Even-money Plus odds	0.8%
With Double Odds	Even-money plus odds	0.6%
Place Numbers		
4 or 10	9-5	6.67%
5 or 9	7-5	4.0%
6 or 8	7-6	1.52%
Buy the 4 or 10	2-1 (-5% commission)	4.76%
Lay Bet against 4 or 10	1-2 (-5% commission)	2.44%
Lay Bet against 5 or 9	2-3 (-5% commission)	3.23%
Lay Bet against 6 or 8	5-6 (-5% commission)	4.0%
Big Six and Big Eight	Even-money	9.09%
Field Bet		
(2-1 paid on both 2 and 12)	Even-money or 2-1	5.55%
(3-1 paid on either 2 or 12)	Even-money or 2-1,3-1	2.7%
Propositions Bets		
Any 7	4-1	16.67%
Any Craps	7-1	11.1%
2 or 12	30-1	13.89%
	30 for 1	16.67%
3 or 11	15-1	11.1%
	15 for 1	16.67%
Hardway 4 or 10	7-1	11.1%
Hardway 6 or 8	9-1	9.09%
Hop Bet	30-1	13.89%
	30 for 1	16.67%

8. YOUR TABLE IMAGE

Introduction

A craps dealer once told me "the game is a great leveler. When you see a guy going crazy at the table and losing everything, the bastard can be a doctor, a judge, a lawyer, whatever, but to us he turns into nothing. Just another loser."

That's an image you don't ever want to have at the craps table. Whenever I play, I get respect from the dealers and the floormen. In order to get respect, I keep my table image solid.

In games like poker, it's important to have a table image that is powerful, for you're playing a game where psychology plays a major part. Even in craps, where everyone is on his or her own, it's still important. It can not only make you a winner, but get you all kinds of comps such as free rooms, free meals, free shows.

Playing Tough

The thing you want to project is the image of tough player. That's the biggest compliment an experienced crew of craps dealers can give to a player - he's a *tough player*.

Tough in this instance means making good bets so that you don't just get your bankroll swept away by a run of bad luck. For example, a foolish player will cover all the place numbers right after the come-out roll, when a pass-line point has been established. Then, after a roll or two, the shooter sevens-out, and all the money is quickly swept away. The player then does the same thing, only this time increasing his pass-line and place bets to make back his losses in a hurry. This is called **chasing**, and it's the downfall of most gamblers. They chase a loss with bigger bets, only to lose those as well.

And that's exactly what happens. The next shooter quickly sevens-out, and the shooter after him falls to the same fate. Before another shooter is ready to come-out, the gambler who's been chasing is out of cash, and while he figures out a way to get fresh gambling money, this shooter goes on a terrific tear with a hot roll. I've seen it happen time and time again.

The tough player, however, doesn't fight the dice. If he's betting with the dice, for them to pass, and they're ice-cold, he keeps his bets to a minimum. He makes only pass-line and come bets, all with double odds, all giving the house a minimum edge. When he's at an ice-cold table, he's preserving his capital in this way. He limits his come bets to two - he waits till the dice turn before increasing his bets and his come wagers.

Never chase your losses. Don't increase bets when losing. Only when winning. Go with the flow, as they say; don't fight the dice. Don't chase.

Table Savvy

There are other ways to enhance your table image. You want to show the casino employees that you know what you're doing. When you come to the table with cash, lay it on the layout; don't hand it directly to the dealer. Tell him what you want. The experienced player calls $5 chips, **nickels**. $25 chips are called **quarters**. In fact, those in the know don't call casino chips, chips. They call them **checks**.

If you have credit at the casino, just tell the dealer you want $500 or $1,000 or whatever. He'll call over a floorman who'll ask your name, and then will check your credit with the pit clerk, who'll look it up on the computer. Those with experience, when the floorman asks how much they want, don't speak. They simply raise one hand and extend their fingers when they want $500. Or show both hands when they want $1,000.

Once you've established credit with the casino, you can ask to be comped for a lot of things, including rooms, beverages, meals - the whole works. Later on, we'll show you how to establish various kinds of credit, including the right to cash personal checks at the casino.

The fun thing about craps is that you can let yourself go at the table. In most other games, there's a subdued atmosphere. But at the craps table you can yell and scream and carry on. When the dice get hot and there are tons of bets on the layout, everytime another good number is rolled, the players at the table whoop and holler and carry on. That's allowed and encouraged. It's the only casino game where this kind of noise level is tolerated. So, get out your inhibitions at the table. It won't hurt your image at all.

After you get your casino checks, put them in the rails in front of your position at the table. Keep an eye on them and protect your chips at all times. They're your responsibility. There are thieves in casinos who prey on busy craps tables. While all the players are paying attention to the dice bouncing around on the table, these guys (or women) are busy snatching players' chips from the rails during those moments when all eyes are on the dice.

Also, if possible, situate yourself at the table so that you can comfortably make your bets. If you're a wrong bettor, making a series of Don't Come wagers, try and stand near the Don't Come box close to the end of the place numbers. On one side it will be near the 4, on the other the 10. This way you can put in the Don't Come bets yourself instead of constantly handing them to the dealer.

Make certain that you have made your bets before the roll. Notice the statement on the layout *No Call Bets*. This means that oral bets are barred. The chips have to be on the table.

This rule is not strictly enforced, however. For example, let's say you come to the table with cash, and while the boxman is counting and verifying its amount, a shooter is about to come-out. You want to get a $25 bet on the pass-line. You can tell the dealer you want to bet $25 this way, and he'll tell you the bet is covered, even though no chips are placed down. Then, after the roll, if it's a winner, you'll get paid off. If it's a craps, for example, he'll subtract $25 from the chips you were supposed to get for your cash.

Establishing a Good Relationship with Dealers

Speaking of dealers, you want to establish a good relationship with them. If you do, they'll be on your side, and sometimes will make you money by reminding you to make an odds bet on the pass-line or on a Come bet. You can tell the dealer you want to bet in a certain way - and he'll make certain that all of the bets you make, even if you forget to do something, will be covered. For example, you can tell him you will make double-odds bets on all the Come numbers.

Let's say you forgot to cover a number. He can remind you just as the roll is made, and will pay you off even if you haven't already handed him the chips. On the other hand, you have to be decent about it, and pay him the odds bet if the shooter sevens-out.

Sometimes, when I've played, after a long time at the table, I'd make a couple of minor mistakes. But if I had a good relationship with the dealer, he'd help me out and in the end, make me money. I remember once betting $300 on the pass-line after the shooter had made two points already. The point was a 5, and I put down $500 as a double-odds bet. The dealer quickly pointed out to me that I could bet $600, and I just as quickly put down another $100 behind the line as a 5 was immediately rolled.

Treat the dealer as a human being. He'll respond. He has a hard job, especially at a crowded table, where every-one is betting heavily. He can make mistakes. Sometimes the mistakes will be in your favor, sometimes not. Don't be too hard on him; he's doing the best he can. When the dealer told me I could bet another $100, it meant $150 more in profits to me.

Therefore I wanted to reward him. The best reward is to tip or toke the dealer. The crew splits all the tips and they're greatly appreciated, since they form the bulk of the dealers income. So let's talk about toking the dealers a bit.

Toking the Dealers

There's nothing written in granite or stone saying you must tip the dealers. But if they're friendly and helpful I feel you should tip them. What amount? That depends. If you're losing, then not much. Dealers understand this. It's hard to part with money while losing. But if you're winning, a small percentage is ok. Let's say you won $100. You can throw four $1 chips out on the table, and say "all the hardways for the boys."

Some crews prefer these kinds of bets, even though they know the odds are against them winning, but if they win, they get 7-1 or 9-1, and they can win all four if luck is with them. Even if they win two, one at 7-1 and one at 9-1, they've taken in $16, and can keep the dollar on each, still working. With a hot roll and pairs coming up on the point and Come numbers, the crew can win a bit of money from the four $1 chips you've thrown out on the table.

Other dealers would prefer the chips given directly to them, while others might want a more secure bet, like a pass-line wager. What I do is ask the dealer working with me - "I'm going to make a bet for the boys. What bet do you want me to make?" And then I"ll make whatever bet he suggests, even if he wants me to bet on the 12 on the next roll. It's up to him.

The Vegas dealers have terms for good tokers. They call them *Georges*. The stiffs they call *Toms*, as in *Tom Turkey*. Some Georges have been very kind to dealers. There is the story of an automobile dealer in Vegas who, after a tremendous session at the table, gave each of the crew a new car.

Toms are more common. They leave with a $10,000 win, with the dealers doing all they can to help, and don't even bother to toke the dealer. If a dealer has cost me money by this indifference or incompetence, then I might not toke him at all. Especially if he's indifferent and bored by my presence. Another dealer I never tip is one who pushes for tokes.

I was once at a Strip casino, and my dealer kept suggesting I make a hardway bet for the boys. After the fifth suggestion, I told him I'd report him to the pitboss and if he did nothing, to the casino manager. I was really getting annoyed. So he shut up. He had spoiled the game for me, however, and since the table was neither hot nor cold, and I was winning but a few bucks, I left the casino altogether.

I can't give you an exact percentage that you should toke the dealers. Use your discretion. If you win a couple of thousand bucks, a bunch of $5 chips or a couple of $25 chips is plenty. Some dealers who are greedy would love to have 10% of your winnings, but hey, when you lose, they're not giving up their tokes to bail you out. Tip moderately, and tip if you've been given good service by the dealers.

Handling and Throwing the Dice

When the dice are passed to you so that you can begin your shoot, you select two of them and the stickman will pull the rest back to him. Before making your first throw you're required to make either a pass-line or don't pass bet. Most shooters will bet pass-line, while very few will bet against their roll by wagering on the don't pass line.

After making a minimum wager on the line, you're not required to make any other bets. In a casino where the minimum line bet is $1, I've seen players bet $1, hold the dice for fifteen minutes before they made their point, and in the interim other players were betting hundreds of dollars on Come and place numbers and winning them.

Then the same shooter made his point, and put another $1 on the pass-line. All in all he held the dice for close to an hour, and while the other gamblers must have taken $75,000-$100,000 off the table as winnings, the shooter ended up winning about $5. That happens.

At other times, the shooter, full of excitement as numbers repeat, inspires a whole table with his enthusiasm and screaming with each roll of the dice. *Four*, he'll scream, then *five. Four again, you little devil you.* And so forth. That table won close to $200,000 for the players as he held the dice for over fifty minutes without throwing more than two 7s, both on the come-out after making his points.

When picking up the dice, do it with one hand, not two. The casino bosses get paranoid when you put a die in each hand. That's the easiest way to switch dice, and they don't like it. Put the dice in one hand and shake that hand or merely throw the dice. Many players, before tossing the cubes, like to twirl them on the surface of the layout, putting them on certain numbers. They may like numbers like 7 and 11 before the come-out, and after that, any number but a 7 or craps. It's up to the individual.

One player I knew had the idea, after practicing for hours at home, that if he set the dice at 6-6, he wouldn't roll a 7. So, for his first number, he just threw the dice at random, then, after the point was established, he covered all the place numbers heavily, and set the dice at 6-6, picked them up carefully and threw them. You can guess the rest. He sevened-out right away.

You must hold the dice in one hand when throwing them, not one in each hand. You also can't rub the dice against your shirt or any part of your body. If you want to rub the dice, let them rub against the felt surface of the layout. And never take them out of view of the table. The boxman will turn purple.

When throwing them, aim them for the far side of the table with sufficient force, so that they both hit the foam covered wall, and take a random bounce. Of course, you want that random bounce if you're legit. There are cheats who practice controlling one die so it skids along the surface, coming up with the same number it started with. The other die rolls and bounces and hits the opposing wall and falls away to a random number.

Cheating

If a cheat can perfect this technique, he has a big edge over the house. For example, on the come-out, he bets heavily on the pass-line, and has one die skid along, starting and ending as a 5. That's his best choice, for he can't roll a craps with a 5 showing on one die. Thus, he has no fear of a 2, 3 or 12.

On the other hand, his 5 gives him two chances for an instant win. If he gets a 2 or 6 on the other die, he gets a natural, that is, a 7 or 11, for a win. He's not only eliminated any chance of losing on the come-out, but he's given himself two out of six ways to win instantly.

That's a terrific shot.

Let's assume this cheat hasn't rolled a 7 or 11, but his point is now 8, with the dice showing 5-3. Now he makes a big odds bet behind his point number, makes huge place number wagers on the 9 and 10, and sets one die at 6. Only an ace on the other die will destroy him, while a 2, 3 or 4 will give him a big profit immediately. He can also make a big bet on the 11, despite the bad odds, now covering four of the five possible numbers that can come up on the random die. Only a 1 will kill him; the 6 will not count one way or another, since the 12 doesn't affect any of his bets.

A cheat might do this for about three rolls, then remove his place bets and his odds bet behind the line, and just roll randomly, hoping to hit his point. If he hasn't hit it in a few rolls, he may once more make a few big place bets and re-establish his odds bet and try again.

It's difficult to accomplish the control of one die, but whole teams of players have descended on craps tables with one player controlling the dice in this manner and destroyed a casino's bankroll in a short period of time.

Thus, as should be evident, the casino prefers that you hit a wall with both dice, with enough force, so that the dice bounce randomly off it and come up with assorted numbers, not with one die coming up the same.

Bad Throws

Occasionally, a player, even though he's not a cheat, will roll the dice poorly, so that one or both never hit a far wall. The boxman can call out immediately, "no roll," if the dice hardly budge from the shooter's hand, or don't cover at least three-quarters of the table. That's up to the boxman. Or he could let it go.

Sometimes beginning players, especially women, have never thrown dice before, and the cubes just seem to fall out of their hands. Generally speaking, the boxman may allow the first roll to stand, but will warn the shooter that unless both dice hit the wall, the throw will not count. What usually ensues is this - the poor lady, frightened to death by this warning, no matter how gently it's applied, will now fling the dice with such force that they fly off the table altogether, after hitting someone at the other end of the table.

Once a die ends up on the rails or off the table in any way, the throw is void and won't count. The game stops till the errant die or dice are found, and then returned to the boxman for examination. After he approves of them, they're generally thrown on the table, along with the dice that the stickman is holding, so that the shooter will select two new dice to throw.

At this point, action usually stops. There are many superstitious players who immediately remove whatever bets they can remove, such as place and odds bets, and wait to see what happens. They worry that the new dice will produce an immediate 7, losing all their bets. Will this happen? I guess so, one time in six. But these players only remember the times it has happened, not the many times it didn't.

If you throw the dice badly, so that only one die hits the

wall, and the other doesn't, the boxman will let the roll slide by, but will warn you to hit the wall with both dice. Maybe warn is too strong a word to use - he'll ask you to throw the dice in a stronger fashion. If you don't heed his advice, he'll disallow the roll or rolls that follow. In the worst case scenario, he'll force you to give up the dice altogether, but this rarely happens.

If a die falls against the wall, so that it doesn't lie flat but is cocked to one side, the side that shows the most surface horizontally will be declared the number thrown on that die. Or if a die jumps on chips and stay there flat, that is also a valid toss, and that number will be counted in the final total of the two dice. Only when a die goes off the table will the roll be absolutely invalid. If one die is off the table and the other shows a number, the roll is null and void. A shooter will have to throw both dice, not just one, to make a valid number appear on the dice.

Cheating will rarely happen at a craps table. The casino personnel should be alert enough to spot tampering with the roll of the dice, or the dice themselves. Some cheats will try to switch dice during a roll - putting in their own dice that have been altered.

But with the safeguards of clear dice, casino logos and imprinted numbers, the casino usually takes enough precautions to prevent this from happening.

9. MAKING BETS

Introduction

At a casino craps table, there will be certain bets that you're responsible for, that is, that you must make yourself. There are other wagers that the dealer makes for you after you give him the chips to make the bet. When I write that you give him the chips, keep in mind that you don't work hand to hand, that is, you don't put the chips into his hand. You place them on the layout and tell the dealer just what to do.

Making Line and Odds Bets

You must make your own pass-line and don't pass bets by putting the chips into the correct boxes on the layout. After a point is established, you are again responsible for making the correct odds bets behind the line. With the pass-line wagers you set the chips behind the original bet. With the don't pass bets, you put the chips next to the original don't pass bet, since, if you bet behind the line literally, the chips would wind up in the pass-line box. For example, to correctly make the don't pass free odds bet, let's say you have two $5 chips in the don't pass box and the point is 5. Now you place three $5 chips (if single odds) next to the original wager. You can also bridge the odd chip by leaving a space between the two distinct bets and placing the odd chips across the two sets of chips.

Even if you have made a double free-odds wager and have more than one odd chips, you can still bridge the chips, as follows: Suppose you've bet $10 or two $5 chips on don't pass. The point is 4 and you are allowed to make a double free-odds bet, laying the odds. This means you can bet $40 in chips (40-20) so you place two $5 chips next to your original bet, leaving a little space between them and put an additional $30 in $5 chips across both piles, bridging them. What the house wants to see is the original bet, so that they don't mix them up. After all, it's paying even-money on the original wager and you're laying the odds at less than even-money on the odds bet.

Making Come, Don't Come Bets and Odds Bets

Let's go back to the bets you make yourself. After a point is established on the come-out roll, if you want to make either a Come or Don't Come bet, you put the chips in the appropriate box on the layout. If you're too far away from the Don't Come box, you can tell the dealer to make the bet for you, after you put the chips down in front of you on the layout.

After a Come point number is established, you must have the dealer make the odds bet by putting down chips on the layout and telling the dealer simply "odds." He'll move your chips to the appropriate box and either put the chips on to cover your original bet as a Come wager, or if you've made a Don't Come bet, he will bridge your chips with your original wager.

Making Field, Big 6 and Big 8 Bets

Although we don't recommend you make the bet, you can also place chips in the Field box and the Big 6 and Big 8 betting areas. The odds are stacked in favor of the casino on these bets and we discourage your making these wagers.

Making Place Bets

When making place bets, you have to put your chips on the layout and instruct the dealer as to the way you want the place bets made. For example, you might put down $60 and instruct the dealer to make only two place bets, $30 each on the 6 and 8. Or you might put down $54 if the point isn't a 6 and 8 and ask the dealer to cover all the place numbers (not recommended). He'll then put $10 in the 4, 5, 9 boxes (assuming 10 is the point) and $12 each in the 6 and 8 boxes. If a 6 or 8 is the point, then then all that's needed to cover the remaining place numbers is $52.

You can bet the place numbers in any way you want. You can put $100 on the 5 and $6 on the 6 if you wish to do that. Remember, however, that the best place numbers to bet on are the 6 and 8, at an advantage of 1.52% to the house. All the others give the house 4% and up, much too much to give away.

Making Lay Bets

Laying bets against any or all numbers also requires the help of the dealer. In addition, you have to give him extra chips to make up for the 5% commission charged. When buying the 4 or 10 or both, you also have to pay the dealer immediately upon making the bets.

Making Proposition Bets

All proposition bets are placed by the stickman. There are two ways to get the stickman's attention. First, you can give your own dealer the chips and instruct him as to the bets you desire. "All the hardways," you will say if you want the chips placed on the hard 4, 6, 8 and 10 at the same time.

He'll then give the chips to the stickman. Or you might toss the chips in the direction of the stickman and instruct him directly. But you can't place your chips in the proposition betting boxes by yourself.

Remember that the dealers are there to help you out, so make use of them, and tip them if you find they're really helpful and have a friendly attitude.

10. STORY - A CARIBBEAN SCORE!

I was once playing in the Caribbean, at a small hotel on one of the smaller island there. I had come with a **junket**, a group of gamblers specially invited for the occasion. Everything was free, but you had to bet a certain amount, several thousand dollars in special chips, as your action for the four days of the trip. These chips were separately marked and colored from the regular chips. If you lost your bet, you lost the special chips. If you won your bet, you were paid off in regular chips. It paid to always bet with the special chips, just to get rid of them and fulfill your obligation to the junketmaster.

The casino was small and had only one craps table working most of the time. They opened a second one after dinner, when the gamblers flowed into the casino. There were other games available - blackjack and roulette. Plus plenty of slot machines for the women accompanying the junketeers.

The first night the dice were ice-cold, with no one able to make two points in a row. Maybe the dice were suspect; I didn't know. But I knew I'd go broke fast if I kept betting with the dice, so on the second night I bet wrong, the only player at the table betting don't pass. I got the usual dirty looks from guys screaming for the point while I was silently wishing for the 7.

I won back my losses the second night, and took a break, getting some fresh air by the water, which was just a couple of hundred feet from the casino. When I came back the second craps table was open, and so I went there. The first one was packed solid and pretty silent, with everyone moaning as the 7s kept showing after the point was established.

I bet against the dice. The staff was young, and I could tell, inexperienced. They had trouble figuring out which payouts to make, and the boxman had to guide them. He was from the States, the dealers were local boys. On the layout there was no Come box, which hurt right players who had to make place bets to cash in on a hot roll. I had previously covered only the 6 and 8 when betting right. Now I simply bet don't pass, laid my single odds, and waited, since there was no Don't Come box either.

My dealer spoke with a Caribbean lilt and had a big friendly smile. As I made my first don't pass bet, he straightened out my chips carefully with his long, slender fingers. The shooter rolled a 10. I had bet $50, and now put down another $100 next to the original bet, bridging the odd two chips, each worth $25.

As the dice were passed again to the shooter, my dealer, seeing the bridge, moved his hands over and stacked them all as one pile. I was about to protest, then realized that I now had $150 against the 10, all at 2-1 odds in my favor. The last $100 therefore had changed from laying 2-1, to an even-money bet where I was heavily favored at the 2-1 odds.

The shooter sevened out a short time later, and my dealer paid me $150 for my bet, instead of the correct $50 for the line bet and another $50 at 1-2 on my free-odds bet. Did he do this on purpose? Or merely out of ignorance of how odds bets worked? I didn't know, so I engaged him in conversation as the dice were moved to a new shooter. He was still friendly, still smiling. I guessed he didn't really know how a player laid odds, since everyone else was betting pass-line and taking odds. Those chips behind the original bet he didn't tamper with.

I made a $75 wager on don't pass this time, and the point was 4. Great! I put down $150 next to my original wager and bridged the chips again. As the dealer's eyes scanned the table, he saw my chips in what he took to be disorder, and quickly straightened them out. So now I had $225 out there, to be paid at even-money. And I was paid a few moments later.

The dice came around to me, but I waved them away. No way I was going to hurt this arrangement. The guy to my left picked them up as I put down $100 in $25 chips on the don't pass line. He rolled a 5. I again made my bridge bet with $150 in chips at 2-3. And again they were straightened out by Maurice, the dealer. This time he shook his head and clucked as if to say, "mon, don't you ever learn?"

My neighbor quickly sevened-out. I was really cherry picking now. The dice moved around the table quickly, another ice-cold session. Now two other players at the other end of the table were betting don't pass also, but their odds bets were left alone by a different dealer.

The boxman wasn't even watching me. He was busy with a drunk betting huge amounts at the other end of the table, and he enlisted the stickman to help him keep the drunk under control. Thus he deprived the casino of a set of eyes that should have been watching my side of the table.

There was no floorman in this arrangement, just a pitboss I had met the night before, who was busy with the other table. So I made bigger and bigger bets and kept bridging the bets, and kept having them straightened out by Maurice. It went on and on for an hour. Unlike American casinos, here there were no breaks for the dealers and they didn't move around the table, a dealer going on break, and another taking the stickman's place.

The stickman was the only experienced dealer in the bunch. He kept on with a sly patter, and had the table laughing despite the heavy losses the right bettors were enduring. I kept at my charade, and kept piling up the chips. Now I was betting with and being paid off with $100 chips.

Finally, after another half-hour, some dealer changes were made. Two older men in the costume of the casino came out and replaced Maurice and the other dealer. I lowered my don't pass bet to $25 to see what would happen. The point was 6 and I put $30 next to the $25 bridging the bet with the odd $5 chip. The dealer watched what I did and didn't straighten it out. I lost that bet as the shooter finally made his point.

I took a break from the action after another fifteen minutes and drank some Perrier with lime and waited in the casino, chatting up a young attractive woman. We talked for close to an hour, then Maurice returned to his old stand, and I excused myself and went back to work.

I made a fortune that night. The difficult thing was getting rid of the special chips this casino had issued to its junket members, but I finally got rid of them in the early hours of the morning. I cashed in then, and put a big wad of bills in the hotel safe. Thereafter I was home free, I enjoyed the pleasures of the island, and at night, if Maurice was at his station at the second craps table, I was in action. If not, I left the casino and took long moonlight walks with the young woman, whose name was Maxime. The Ms were lucky for me on that moonlit Caribbean island.

11. HOW TO ESTABLISH CREDIT AT A CASINO

Introduction

If you play craps seriously, you might want to establish credit at a casino. Thus, you won't have to drag large amounts of cash with you everytime you head to Vegas or Atlantic City or wherever there is legitimate casino craps play.

You must fill out an application which the casino provides. It covers a bit of information, but basically, before issuing credit, the casino is interested in your credit history at other casinos. But suppose you don't have any such history; you just want to establish credit at this casino and either go no further, or use it as a springboard for other casinos.

For example, if you establish credit in Atlantic City, you can use this credit history to establish credit in Las Vegas, or vice-versa. However, let's assume you have no credit history. You arrive at the X casino on the Strip in Vegas, and want to work out some credit arrangement for the next time you're at this casino. Here's what you do. You go to the cashier's cage and ask for a credit application.

You fill out the application, leaving blank any other casino credit you might have. What becomes important now is the amount of money your normally keep in your checking account. The casino won't give you more credit than you normally keep in that account. For instance, suppose your average balance in your checking account is less than $1,000. Forget about getting credit in a casino. They usually issue a line of credit from $1,000 and up. How high? I spoke to a credit manager who told me $1,000,000 is not unheard of, and they even go higher, much higher than that for the **whales**, the really big gamblers who will bet $50,000 on each hand. That's big-time gambling in anyone's book.

To prepare for proper credit, you should maintain a balance in your checkbook of well over the figure you're asking for. Suppose you want a credit line of $5,000 in the casino. Then I'd advise you to have a normal balance of $7,000 or more for the last several months. That's what the casino is looking for, and that's what the credit department is going to ask your bank about. What's your average balance in the checking account?

Of course, you don't have to wait to get credit by going directly to the casino. You can do it by phone, fax or mail these days. What you do is simply call the 800 number of the casino you're thinking of visiting, and requesting an application. If you need it in a hurry, they'll fax it to you. You can also apply by phone in many casinos, giving the information about yourself to a representative of the casino. On average, it only takes one day to get credit at a hotel-casino.

This way, by the time you arrive at the front desk, check in, you'll have your credit established. Then it's an easy matter to play. Just go to the craps table, see a floorman and he'll verify your credit line. You can draw from the line for play, as long as you don't exceed your credit line. Then it's shut off.

But if you play according to the precepts outlined in this book, you should do ok. You won't be making outrageous bets and you'll give the house a minimum edge, and that's all you'll be giving them.

If you have credit, and play during your stay, and find yourself winning, when you cash in at the cashier's cage, you'll be asked if you have any markers outstanding. A **marker** is the IOU you'll be signing with the floorman when you request credit. Let's back up a a bit and see how that works.

Markers

You check into a hotel, and go to your room, wash up and relax, then head for the craps tables. You see a table that has a couple of openings, and it looks active. You need a warm table that might heat up into a hot table. Ok. So you move in and stand in an open spot and tell the dealer you want credit. He'll signal a floorman who'll come over to you and ask your name, and how much credit you want.

Let's say you have a $5,000 credit line at the casino, and want to start off with $500. So you tell him $500. The floorman will excuse himself, and go to the pit clerk, who will look you up. Satisfied, the floorman will tell the dealer to give you the $500 in chips. Then, a few minutes later, the floorman will arrive with a marker for you to sign for the $500. You sign it, and now you owe the casino $500.

After an hour of play, you find yourself ahead $700. So you take the $1,200 in chips ($500 + $700 profit) to the cashier's cage. The woman there will ask you if you have any markers outstanding. Tell her the truth - you have one. I say tell the truth because you've established credit with this casino and you might as well be upfront, and start a good relationship. She'll ask you to pay off the marker. So you do this with $500, and the marker will be returned to you, and you can tear it up. You still have your credit line intact.

But let's say have a bad four days in the casino and lose $1,200. You have three $500 markers outstanding, and $300 in cash from the last marker, for you only lost $200 the last time you played. Now you're checking out of the hotel. You should go to the cashier's cage and give them a check for $1,500 to cover the markers and pay them off.

An excuse that you forgot your checkbook won't work.

They'll produce a counter check and have it filled out with the name of your bank. Once you sign this check, you will find that it will be drawn against your checking account.

Keeping Good Credit

There are unscrupulous players who establish credit in a casino, use the credit a few times, then empty their bank accounts, specifically their checking account, and when they issue a check, it bounces. What happens? Well, the casino generally won't sue the player; they'll simply cut off his credit and eat the loss. In the old days of mob dominated casinos, that individual might get paid a visit he'd long remember, and happily he'd fork over the funds he owed. Today, the corporations take the loss.

But that loss will kill the player's credit in every casino in America. His credit rating will be zilch. If he plays craps from then on, it'll be on a cash basis. If he wants to re-establish credit, he can after paying off his debt. But then, for the first few times he plays, he'll have to deposit funds like cash or cashier's checks into his account in the casino. And he can play against these funds.

The casino will be forgiving generally. The only hold they really have on the player is his desire to gamble. If a player reneges on a debt for two years and repays, the casino won't collect interest on the debt. Casino debt is interest free, for the most part.

Use Credit Wisely

Our advice is, establish credit and use it wisely.

If you have a $5,000 credit line with a casino, it costs you nothing in interest and charges. It's much more sane than borrowing $5,000 from your credit card at 19% or more interest. In fact, never borrow money to gamble with - that's asking for big trouble.

If you establish credit at a casino, make sure that you can afford to lose it all. This is not saying you will, but don't gamble with money you can't afford to lose financially. That's also asking for big trouble.

Gambling and shooting dice and playing casino craps can be fun and exciting. Don't let it become anything else. Play sanely and correctly and play to win. Don't play just to have action; that's the wrong approach altogether.

Getting Comped

Pick and choose the casino you want to play at for several good reasons. First of all, it's better to play where double odds is offered, rather than single odds, for that lowers the casino edge on your best bets to 0.6%.

Also, you can shop around by calling the 800 numbers most casinos have. They don't cost you anything, and you can get valuable information. How valuable? Well, while writing this chapter, I called Vegas and spoke to a credit manager of a Strip Hotel. I asked at what level of credit I'd be comped to a free room. She told me $2,500 would entitle me to a free room from Sunday to Wednesday nights. However, my bets would have to be $38-$50 each time.

I called another hotel and found that in order to be comped, I have to have $3,000-$5,000 in credit and bet at least $50 and play four hours a day, or 12 hours for a three-day stay. That's a little more stringent than the first hotel.

Both places are first-class and are internationally known. They both do well. There are other casinos not doing that well. They might comp you to a room for much less play and smaller action. And they might also throw in meals and beverage service.

So, my advice is to shop around and see what the hotels will offer. Remember, it doesn't take long to have your credit verified. Most hotels will do it on one day. That's all. I'm assuming you call or write them during the week. Don't expect to ask them on Friday and get an answer on Saturday. Banks are closed on Saturdays. It might take till Tuesday. Then you're in business.

Rooms in the better hotels cost about $60-$65 a night. More on weekends, depending upon the establishment. Some hotels will charge much more, $100 or more. The question is, is it worth playing twelve hours at $50 a shot just to beat the cost of the room? I think not. After all, a $60 room is just one play plus $10, and you're going to be making a lot of plays per hour. What's one more or less? It's better to be your own man and come and go when you please, and bet as little as you care to. Don't fall into the trap of cadging a free room by making bets you don't want to or can't afford to make.

On weekends, even with that heavy play of $50 per shot, you may only get what is known as "casino rate" on the room. A casino rate is reduced rate. You're not even getting a free room. So then, it's absolutely crazy to give the house that much intensive action, so they'll reduce your room rate by $20.

Use your head in planning your visit. If you're comfortable with $50 a play, if you've got money to spare and make a good living and it won't mean anything to you, and besides, you want to spend that much time at the tables, get the free room while you're at it. If not, pay for your own room.

While playing, if you have credit, the floorman might also extend other comps to you as a goodwill gesture. And there are casino hosts who walk around and make sure that the credit players enjoy themselves. He might give you a free show, a couple of free meals, a bottle of liquor to your room. See how they treat you.

If you don't like the treatment, if they're real cheap about everything, go to another hotel and establish credit there. If you switch from hotel X to hotel Y, having credit at X, you might get very fast service on your credit at Y and you might be able to check into the new hotel during your stay in Vegas or Atlantic City.

Always do what's best for you, whether it's setting sane limits on your gambling or getting something from a hotel-casino you're giving your action to. That's the best advice I can give you.

12. PRINCIPLES OF WINNING PLAY

Introduction

In casino craps, the house holds an edge on all bets made by the player, with the exception of the free-odds wagers allowed on all pass-line, don't pass, Come and Don't Come situations. By making maximum odds bets, the player is able to reduce the edge considerably. In the above situations, a player making any of these wagers is giving the casino a 1.41% edge, if he doesn't make a free-odds wager.

However, by making a single free-odds bet, that 1.41% is reduced to 0.8%. Double free-odds bets reduce it further to 0.6%. When ten times free-odds bets are allowed, we almost have an even game with the casino. We can't always pick a casino with ten times free-odds bets. More likely, we'll be playing in a casino that allows either single or double free-odds. In Atlantic City, for example, expect to play single odds. In Lake Tahoe, expect the same thing.

Vegas gives you a much greater choice, ranging from single to ten times odds. Although the best game by far is one at ten times odds, you might find yourself in a casino that offers double odds. You have credit in that casino, or a room there, and will find it convenient to play there.

Or you live on the East Coast, and Atlantic City is just a couple of hours away, and you don't have the time to book a flight to Vegas and spend three or four days there. Also, you have to take into consideration the roundtrip fare and other expenses. Is all that worth going for double instead of single odds? Not likely.

When discussing winning methods, we'll show how to play in all situations; whether single, double or a ten times odds game. We'll discuss the situations thoroughly, and we'll give you methods to play that are conservative, aggressive and super-aggressive. Surely one of those categories will fit you, the reader. One of them will be comfortable for you.

Our winning methods won't be limited just to those players who bet with the dice. We'll show you how to win betting wrong. We'll give you every kind of situation that you can choose from, with one idea in mind. When the dice go your way, you'll make maximum profits. When the dice go against you, you won't get that hurt. I think that's a great combination. So, let's start at the beginning. The beginning is bets you'll never make at a craps table. By avoiding these wagers, you're halfway to success.

Bets to Avoid

If you follow our advice and don't make any of the bets we suggest you avoid, you'll end up saving yourself a lot of money. Not only that, you'll be classified by experienced pros as a "tough player," a player who knows what he's doing, who's not a sucker. By tough, they also mean a player who's tough to beat.

Avoid all proposition bets in the center of the layout. We've gone over every bet in full, from the horn wager to Any Seven, from the hardways to the Any Craps. They all have one thing in common - they're all bad for your bankroll, since they give the house an edge ranging at minimum of 9.09% all the way up to 16.67%. Who needs to give this much away? Not us, certainly.

The only possible bet you might make in the center of

the layout is a hardway bet, *only as a toke for the dealers.* Make it if the dealer requests it. If he wants another bet made or wants the toke directly, then there's no reason to make a hardway bet.

And never think about protecting your pass-line wagers with an Any Craps wager that gives away 11.1%. You're only protecting the casino's profits when you make this bet. OK, we have this straight. We never never never make a center proposition wager.

Let's move on from there. We never make a Big 6 or Big 8 bet anywhere but in Atlantic City. We only make it in Atlantic City under limited circumstances, as will be shown in our betting strategies, that is, in multiples of $6 if we are paid 7-6 for our wager. If we are only paid even-money, forget it! In fact, why even make it in Atlantic City? If you want to place bet the 6 and 8, let the dealer handle it with the place numbers.

Anywhere else you're only getting even-money for the Big 6 and Big 8, on a bet that should pay 6-5. This gives the casino a 9.09% edge. They don't deserve it, and don't give it to them. Avoid these wagers.

The Field Bet is another one to avoid. Where the 2 and 12 are both paid off at 2-1, the house edge is 5.55%. Much too much. Where the 2 or 12 is paid off at 3-1, with the other at 2-1, the house advantage drops to 2.7%. Not bad but not good. We don't want to give up that amount to any casino. We never want to give up more than 1.52%, and that only under certain conditions. But that's it. Never more than that, and the Field Bet takes more, so we avoid the wager.

That leaves a few other wagers. Lay bets, which are bets against particular numbers, are rarely made, but don't you be the one to make it. The best of these wagers gives up more than 2%. Remember our admonition. We don't give up more than 1.52%. So forget about lay wagers.

Now we come to the bets that are very popular and that destroy more craps players than any others. These are the place number bets. When we make a place bet on the 4 and 10, instead of getting the correct 2-1 payout, we only get 9-5. This gives the casino a nice 6.67% cut as their edge. Even if we buy these same numbers by paying a 5% commission in order to get a correct 2-1 payout, we're still giving away 4.76% to the house. Don't make these wagers. They'll eat you up alive in the long run. In the short run you can sometimes get lucky, but that never lasts as the law of large numbers, often called mistakenly the law of averages, catches up to you.

Now we move on to the 5 and 9 as place numbers. They pay off at 7-5 instead of the correct 3-2. That's a big difference, taking 4% out of your pocket. It's too much to give up. Don't make a place bet on the 5 and 9.

The 6 and 8 should be paid off at 6-5 as place numbers, but all the house will give us is 7-6. This gives the casino a 1.52% edge, by far the smallest edge on the layout other than the line bets, the Come and Don't Come bets and those combined with free-odds wagers. Still, 1.52% isn't 0.6%. The only time we recommend placing the 6 and 8 is in our super-aggressive betting systems. Otherwise, forget about them.

When we talk about casino advantages on bets, we're not just whistling Dixie, or pounding our chest to show how clever we are about the mathematics behind the bets. They have a realistic basis, in the amount of money these bets cost you in the long run.

When you give the house 9.09% or 11.1% on the hardway bets for example, what this means is - for every $100 you wager, theoretically you'll lose either $9.09 or

$11.11. Hey, that's a big bite out of $100!

On the other hand, betting the line and taking or laying double odds, gives the house 0.6%. What does that translate to in loss expectation? For every $100 you wager you give the house 60¢!!! For 60¢ they're running the game and giving you free drinks and possibly a show or meal thrown in as a comp.

You know what would happen if everyone just made line, Come and Don't Come bets and took or laid double odds? The casinos would close up their craps games. They couldn't make enough to pay the employees working the tables and all the other personnel that backs up the operation. So, when we talk about house edges, think about that $100 and what your loss expectation is. That's a better and clearer way to take a look at the big picture that odds and advantages mean to you.

So, after telling you what not to bet on, this leaves the line bets, the pass-line and don't pass, the Come and Don't Come wagers. It leaves the free-odds wagers as well, and in the super-aggressive systems, the place numbers 6 and 8. Everything else is swept away. A good analogy is the roulette table. When a number comes up, all the other losing chips are just swept out of sight, except for a few supporting the winning number. It's the same with craps. You are now focussed only on a few bets. Nothing else matters.

No matter how charming the stickman is, no matter how honey-toned his vocal cords get in asking you to bet the "hardways, bring out the point," or "craps eleven," "get those bets down," no matter what he pleads with you to do, it's all no good. Get your focus in tight, and never lose track of what can win for you. Those few good bets and nothing else.

Now let's get to our first betting system.

13. WINNING STRATEGIES: BETTING RIGHT

Introduction

The first group of strategies will be for those players who bet right, or with the dice. First, let's cover a conservative approach that's very strong for the player.

This strategy can be played at either a single or double free-odds casino. Let's first discuss the single odds game.

CONSERVATIVE
1. Single Odds - Conservative

When playing at a casino that permits only single-odds free-odds bets, you should endeavor to make a three-unit bet as your pass-line wager. You do this for one good reason - it enables you to bet even more than single-odds behind the line on certain points. This reduces the house edge below 0.8%. Anytime we reduce the house advantage, we're doing the right thing. We're playing tough.

So, here's how the betting system works.

1. We make a pass-line wager of three units. I don't care what the three units are - they can be $1, $5, $25 or $100 or even more. It depends upon your bankroll and your ability to handle big wagers. Let's assume we're an average bettor and wager $15, three units of $5 each.

2. As soon as a point is established, we make the maximum free-odds wager allowed. If the point is 4 or 10, all we can wager is an additional three units behind the line at 2-1 odds. If the point is 5 or 9, we're permitted to wager four units or $20 as a free-odds wager at 3-2. If the point is a 6 or 8, we can wager five units or $25 behind the line at the correct odds of 6-5.

The enhanced free-odds allowed on the 5 or 9 and 6 or 8 is why we start with a three-unit wager.

3. We now make a Come wager of three units, so as to catch the enhanced free-odds on this bet also. Whatever the Come point, we take maximum odds again. This means three units on the 4 and 10, four units on the 5 and 9 and five units on the 6 and 8.

4. We now make another Come wager and again take the maximum free-odds allowed by the house.

5. After we've established a pass-line point and two Come points, we stop betting. We have three numbers working for us at this time, giving away no more than 0.8% to the house.

6. If a Come number repeats and we're paid off, we make one more Come bet, and again take the maximum odds. We always want to have two Come numbers as well as the pass-line point working for us.

7. If the pass-line point is made, we make another pass-line wager, again taking the maximum free-odds. If the pass-line point rolled is the same as one of our Come points, we make another Come bet, keeping the three numbers working at all time.

For example, to make this perfectly clear, suppose that originally the pass-line point was a 5, and the two Come point numbers were 4 and 8. The shooter makes his 5 and there's a new come-out roll. He rolls a 4 as his point. Since the 4 was one of our Come numbers, we're paid on the original bet (the odds bets on Come numbers don't work on the come-out) and the 4 is taken down.

Now we only have the 4 as a pass-line number and the 8 as a Come number. So we must make another wager on the Come, to re-establish two Come numbers.

That's the basic system for the conservative bettor. It can be enhanced in the following way.

2. Enhanced Conservative Approach

Add step 8 to the seven steps of the above approach:

8. After any two payoffs, either Come or pass-line, increase the original bet by one unit. After two more payoffs, increase the original bet by another unit. And keep doing this after each two payoffs from then on.

Thus, suppose in the above example, after the 5 was repeated as a pass-line winner, the shooter now threw an 8. That is a winner on the Come number 8, and the 8 is taken down and we're paid off. The 8 is our pass-line point and we have the 4 as a Come point.

Now, we have to make another Come bet. But instead of betting only three units, we bet four units on the Come. Let's say the next roll is a 6. The 6 is a Come point now. We'd be allowed to bet five units on the free-odds bet. Let's assume that the shooter now makes the 8. We make a four unit bet on the pass-line. If the point is a 10, we bet four units behind the ten at 2-1. Then the shooter makes the 6 and it comes down. Another two repeats of any point numbers and we make a five-unit Come wager. And so on.

In this way, during a hot roll, we are increasing our bets slowly, and winning a bunch of money with the enhanced wagers. We're taking the roll as it comes; we're not antici-pating anything. This is much saner than the approach of many craps gamblers who press or double their bets after each win, only to find that final 7 losing all their previous hard-earned winnings.

Enhanced Sample Shoot

Let's now follow a previous roll in its entirety, in terms of money bets and money paid out to us.

First, we've established the 5 as a pass-line point, the 4 and the 8 as Come points. That means an outlay of $45 in original bets and $20 on the 5 as a free-odds wager, $15 on the 4, and $25 on the 8 as free-odds bets. We now have a total of $105 out on the table.

At this moment, before the next roll of the dice, we're most vulnerable to a complete loss. This will happen occasionally. When it happens time and time again, we've run into a buzzsaw of bad luck. But the chances are in our favor that it won't happen; that instead we'll get some payoffs before that 7 shows.

The 5 is made by the shooter. We collect the following: $15 on the line bet plus $30 on the free-odds wager.

Total win so far: $45

We now bet $15 on the pass-line. *The shooter rolls a 4 on the new come-out.* The 4 is our new pass-line point. We bet $15 behind the line on the 4 at 2-1. We collect $15 for our Come bet on the 4 (odds are off on the come-out.)

Total win: $60

The shooter now gets ready to roll, and we make a Come bet of four units, since two numbers have already been made. *A 6 is rolled*, and we have four units on the 6 as a Come bet and five-units as a free-odds wager. We now have the 4 as a pass-line point with the 6 and 8 as Come bets. *The shooter repeats his pass-line point of 4.* We collect the following: $15 on the original bet and $30 on the free odds wager.

Total win: $105

Now we make a four-unit wager on the pass-line and *the shooter rolls a 10.* We make another four-unit wager behind the line. The 10 is our pass-line point. *The shooter rolls a 6* which wins our Come bet. We collect the following: $20 as our Come bet and $30 as our free-odds wager.

Total Win: $155

We now make a five-unit wager on the Come, and *the shooter sevens out.* We collect the following: $25 as our Come bet.

Total Win: $180

But we lose the following:
$20 on the pass-line bet and $20 on the pass-line free-odds bet on the 10. $15 on the Come bet of the 8, and $25 for the free-odds wager.

Total losses: $80

NET WIN: $100

Conservative Approach Summary

We can see that, by establishing two Come numbers only and keeping them working, we leave ourselves with little exposure to the 7 showing. There are only certain times when the 7 will really hurt. And by increasing our bets slowly, we again don't expose too much to a big loss when the 7 is rolled. And we still can take advantage of a roll that has repeating numbers in it.

Make a simplified layout at home, using the pass-line, Come and place number boxes, and use ordinary chips or coins as your betting units. Throw the dice and follow this system for a number of rolls. See how comfortable you are with it, and if you feel it works for you, by all means get it down pat, and try it in a casino setting.

If $5 units are too large for your comfort, either financially or emotionally, try $1 units. There are plenty of places where you can bet $1 at the tables, especially in Nevada. Thus, you can take the chance of winning a big score without putting too much money at risk.

If you don't want to make three-unit bets, then you can bet one unit to begin with. Let's assume you bet $5. We don't recommend $1 because you can't take odds on the 6 and 8.

If you bet $5, then take single odds, and make Come bets of $5 with single odds. After two repeats, you can increase your $5 bet to $10, or you can go more gradually, by increasing it $2 or $3. Do whatever is comfortable for you - the system is very efficient and yet very flexible.

3. Double Odds Strategy - Conservative

When double odds are offered, we don't have to bet three-units at a time to grab the enhanced odds available with the 5 or 9 and 6 or 8. We get double odds on everything, so we can start with two-units. Of course, if you want to start with three-units that's fine. Or one-unit. That's fine also. Our system will analyze the two-unit game, however.

Here's how we play the double odds game.

1. We make a two-unit pass-line wager and then, after the point is established, we make a free-odds bet double the original wager.

2. We make a Come bet of the same two-units. When that point is established, we make a double odds bet of that Come point.

3. We make another Come bet of two-units and back it up with a double odds wager. Having three numbers working for us, one pass-line and two Come points, all with double odds, we stop betting.

At this point, assuming we're betting with $5 chips, we have $30 out as underlying wagers, and $60 as free-odds bets. The house advantage over us is a measly 0.6%.

4. If a Come number repeats, it is taken down and we make another Come bet to re-establish the three numbers that we want working. If a pass-line is repeated, we make another pass-line wager. If the new pass-line point is one of our Come numbers, we make another Come bet. As always, we want three numbers working for us.

5. After two wins of repeating pass-line or Come numbers or any combination of them, we increase our underlying bet on the next wager by one-unit. Now we're betting three units and putting up six units as our free-odds wager.

6. After two more wins, we again increase our underlying by by one-unit and again take double odds. We continue to do this after each two wins of repeating Come and pass-line points only. We don't count an 11 coming up either on the pass-line or as a Come winner. Nor do we count losers such as a craps, whether it comes up on the pass-line or Come. It's the two repeating numbers that allow us to increase the wagers by one unit.

Let's follow a sequence of rolls to see how this works out.

Double Odds Shoot

We bet two-units, or $10 on the pass-linc and the *shooter comes-out with a 7*. A winner for us of $10.
Total Win: $10

The next roll is a 3. A $10 loser on the pass-line.
Total Win: $0

On the next come-out *the shooter rolls a 6*. We place $20 behind the line at 6-5 correct odds. We now make a Come wager of $10. *The next roll is an 8*. We place $20 as a free-odds bet and make another Come bet of $10. The shooter rolls a 2, a loser for us.
Total Loss: $10

We make another Come bet, still looking for that third working number. *The next roll is a 9*. We put $20 out as a free-odds wager at 3-2. Now that we have three numbers working, we stop betting. *The next two rolls are 4 and 3*, which don't affect us at all. *Then the shooter rolls an 8*. This is a winner for us of $34 ($10 + $24 odds win.)
Total Win: $24

Now we make another Come bet of $10. *The shooter rolls a 6*, a winner as a pass-line point. But we also establish the 6 as a Come bet and give the dealer $20 as a free-odds bet. We collect $34 for the pass-line win on the 6.
Total Win: $58

We now have both the 6 and 9 as come numbers, as the shooter prepares to come-out again. We now place three-units on the pass-line, since two points have been repeated. *The shooter rolls a 7*. It's a $15 win for us on the pass-line.

Total Win: $73

However, we lose both of our $10 underlying bets on the 8 and 9 for a loss of $20.
Total Loss: $20

Net Win: $53

Double Odds Summary

Since it was a come-out, our odds bets were returned to us because they're not working on the come-out roll. Now the shooter prepares for another come-out roll and we again make a three-unit wager on the pass-line. The shooter will have to repeat two more points before we raise this wager to four-units. Remember, we don't count the 7 as a winner in raising our unit bets.

We're going to show one more conservative approach before moving on to an aggressive betting system.

4. Ten Times Odds - Conservative Approach

The Horseshoe and a few other casinos in Las Vegas may have this option when you get there. They will allow you to bet *ten times odds* as a free-odds bet. This is the best deal you have as a craps player. It's almost an even game with the house.

1. Make a one-unit wager, then, after the point is established, make a ten-times odds bet.
2. Make a Come bet, and after the Come point is established, make a ten-times odds bet.
3. Make a second Come bet and after this point comes up, make a ten-unit free odds bet. Having three numbers working for you, you stop betting and wait to see what happens.

Assuming you've been betting $5 chips, you'd have $55 on each point, or a total of $165. This is quite a large sum, despite the almost nonexistent edge the house has on your bets.

If you're uncomfortable with that level of betting, some casinos allow a bet as low as $1, so you can start with a $2 bet. With three numbers covered and ten-times odds, this comes to $66. If you bet $3 as your basic bet, then you'd put out $99.

Since ten times bets makes the bets escalate rather rapidly, we suggest the following:

4. After two points have been repeated, if you started with $2, raise the bet to $3 as an underlying bet. If you started with $3, raise it to $4. If you started with $5, raise it to $7. Then after each two wins as repeating numbers show up, increase by $1 if you started with $2 or $3, and increase by $2 if you started with $5.

None of this is written in stone. If you want to really take a plunge, you can increase the underlying bet by more than what we have suggested. Or, if you worry about the escalation of the odds bets, you can hold back increasing the bets until three numbers have repeated.

But once those numbers repeat, with ten-times odds, you're going to get some mighty powerful payouts. Let's say you bet $5 and took $50 odds on both a 4 and a 9, and they repeated. You'd collect $105 on the 4 and $75 on the 9. It can really add up. If you have the money and the nerve, ten-times betting is the way to go for really huge wins.

Conservative Approach Conclusion

On the other hand, you're risking some big bucks when you've established those three numbers, and they're naked out there for a 7 to wipe them out. But that's what craps is all about, nerve, excitement and the chance for a big score or bad losses if the dice go against you.

But always remember, making ten-times wagering as free-odds gives the house the absolute minimum edge and in the long run, this tiny advantage can lead you to some big wins.

This concludes the Conservative Approach to betting systems. Study them carefully, and as suggested before, practice them at home with a makeshift layout, some chips or coins and a pair of dice. See which one you're most comfortable with, which one works best for you.

AGGRESSIVE APPROACH
5. Introduction

With the Conservative Approach, we limited our come bets to two only, for the more Come bets out, the greater the chance of that 7 coming up on the dice and wiping them out. However, the converse is true, also. The fewer the Come bets, as each one is repeated, the more they have to be established, and with a long, hot roll, the profit potential is increased with more Come bets being bet.

For example, suppose the pass-line point is 5, and we've established only two Come bets, the 9 and 6. The 9 is repeated, and now we make another Come bet and another 9 is rolled. Instead of two payouts if we had kept a third Come bet going, we only have one. Here's how we calculated the difference.

Suppose, after the Come bets 9 and 6 were established, we made another Come wager. Now, if the 9 is thrown, repeating our original 9 Come bet, we get paid the under-lying bet and maximum free-odds. However, we still have the 9 working, for it's *off and on*, with our 9 Come bet still intact.

6. The Off and On Strategy

If we did it in slow-motion, here's what happens. The 9 Come bet is paid off but not taken down, because of the Come bet in the Come box. Thus, we get a payout, the underlying Come bet in the 9 box is left on with the free-odds bet, and the Come bet we made in the Come box is also left in the Come box. In other words, except for the payoff to us, everything stays the same. We still have a Come bet plus free-odds in the 9 box, and we still have our bet in the Come box. Now, if another 9 is rolled, as in our example, we have the same situation. We have gotten two payoffs on the 9, still establish the 9 as a Come bet, still have a Come bet working.

If we made only two Come bets and stopped, we'd get only one payout, for the 9 Come bet and free-odds would be taken down, and we'd have to make another Come bet to re-establish the 9, which was rolled next.

The difference is this - we have continuous Come bets working with three instead of two Come bets made, as, if there's a double repeat of a number, which happens from time to time, we get extra payouts. I've personally had the Come bet on a 6 go *off and on* five times in a row, and I was increasing my wager on the Come box after two repeats. I started with two $25 chips, and thus had a $50 bet out. The 6 was established as a Come point and I gave the dealer $100 as a double free-odds wager.

Then I made another $50 come bet. This was the second Come bet after the come-out, the first being the 6. A 10 was rolled, and I gave the dealer $100 as a free-odds bet. The pass-line point was an 8.

So, right then, I had $50 + $100 on the 8 as a pass-line wager, and $50+$100 on the 10 and $50+$100 on the 6. I then made another $50 Come bet and a 6 was rolled. I was paid $50 + $120 for a $170 payout.

My $50 remained in the come box, and another 6 was rolled. I collected another $170 and now put $75 in the Come box. Another 6 came up. I received another $170 and now gave the dealer $150 as a free-odds bet. Another 6 was rolled. I now collected $75 + $180 for a $225 payout. I had another $75 in the Come box because the roll was *off and on* and the fifth 6 came up. I collected $75 + $180, and still had the 6 as a Come bet. I now had collected $170 + $170 + $170 + $255 + $255 for a total of $1,020.

I put $100 in the Come box, and now the shooter rolled an 8, winning the pass-line bet. So I collected $170 more. I put $100 in the pass-line betting area for the new come-out and the shooter rolled a 7. I won another $100 for the pass-line bet, and lost $100 on the 8 and $50 for the 10.

All in all, my net winnings on that short, but intense roll was $1,140, because of the repeating 6s. The extra Come bet enabled me to keep collecting without interrupting the flow and re-establishing the 6 every other roll.

7. Single Odds - Aggressive Approach

1. We make a pass-line wager of three-units, and after the point is established, we take the maximum free-odds allowed. To refresh your recollection, if the point is a 4 or 10, you put three chips behind the line, if it's a 5 or 9 you place four chips behind the line, and if the pass-line point is a 6 or 8, you bet five chips behind the line.

2. We now make a Come bet of the same three-units, again taking the maximum odds allowed.

3. We make a second Come bet of three-units with maximum free-odds.

4. We make a third Come bet with maximum free odds allowed. Our purpose is to have three Come bets and a pass-line wager point working for us - in other words, four numbers. This won't always happen, because the Come and pass-line points may repeat themselves during this betting scheme.

5. If there are two repeats of points, either come or pass-line points, then we increase our underlying bets by two units to five units. For example, if we've been betting $15, we increase it to $25, and take the maximum free-odds allowed.

6. After each repeat after that, we increase our underlying betting unit by one more unit, and keep doing this, as well as taking maximum free-odds. We are always striving to have three Come numbers working for us.

7. Should we have three Come numbers working, then we stop betting till there's a repeat of one of the Come numbers, and we then make the appropriate bet in the Come box. If a pass-line point repeats, we make another pass-line bet. The amount we bet depends on what happened before.

For example, suppose we follow a shoot to see how this works.

Sample Shoot: Aggressive Single Odds

The shooter is you, for once. You make a $15 bet on the pass-line *and roll a 7*. A winner.

Total Win: $15

Now you have another come-out roll. *You roll another 7.*
Another winner!
Total Win: $30

You still make a $15 wager on the pass-line. You must
repeat two points to increase your bets. 7s don't count. We
make this rule because when there's a point, there's an
odds bet as well, so more is at stake. We need a couple of
big wins before we increase our wagers.

You now roll a 4 as your come-out point. You place $15
behind the line, as your free-odds bet. You put $15 in the
Come box and *roll an 8.* You give the dealer $25 as your
free-odds bet at 6-5. You put another $15 in the Come box
and *roll a 9.* You give the dealer $20 as a free-odds wager at
3-2. Since you only have two Come numbers working, you
again put $15 in the Come box and *roll another 9.* The bet
is *off and on* and you collect $45.
Total Win: $75

You still have $15 in the Come box and *now roll a 10.* You
give the dealer $15 as a free-odds bet at 2-1 on the 10. At this
moment in time, you have the 4 as a pass-line point, and the
8, 9 and 10 as Come points, all with free-odds to the max.
Therefore you stop making Come bets.

You shake the dice and throw them, *you roll an 11.* It
doesn't count for you. *You roll a 3.* Again, a no-counter. *You
roll a 5.* You don't have that number covered so it's a wasted
roll. You really shake the dice and *roll an 8.* OK! You are
paid $45 for the 8, which is taken down as a Come number
since you didn't have a bet in the Come box. You now bet
$25 in the Come box, because you've had two numbers
repeat, the 9 and 8. *You now roll a 4,* making your point on
the pass-line. You're paid $45 for the 4, which goes with the

$45 you were paid for the 8 before.
Total Win: $165

You give the dealer $25 as an odds bet on the 4 which is now a Come point, to go along with the 9 and 10, all outside numbers, all difficult to make. Now you make a $25 bet in the pass-line box. You shake the dice and *roll a 9.* Damn, the 9s are good to you. You collect $15 for the 9 and the odds bet is returned to you.
Total Win: $180

You make a $30 wager as an odds bet at 3-2 on the 9. Since you only have two Come bets out, on the 4 and 10, you make another $25 wager in the Come box. *You roll a 6.* You give the dealer $30 as a free-odds bet. You now have three Come bets working, the 4, 6 and 10, and the 9 is your pass-line point. Don't worry about keeping track of all these numbers. The dealer will be there to help you, and you're standing at a table watching the action and can clearly see what you have covered.
You shake the dice and roll a 3. It doesn't count for you. *You roll an 8.* Again, it doesn't count. *You now roll a 10.* A winner! You collect $45, and make a Come bet of six units, raising your underlying bet by one unit. From now on, after each repeat, you'll increase that bet by one unit.
Total Win: $225
You now roll a 6. It's another winner, and you collect $25 + $36 for the 6, or $61.
Total Win: $286

Now your $30 is given to the dealer, who will allow you to make a $50 free-odds wager. You look around. You have the 4 and 6 as Come bets and the 9 as a pass-line point. You place seven units, or $35 in the Come box. But the dice are tired, *and you seven-out*. You collect another $35 for your Come bet.

Total Win: $321

You lose $80 on the 6, $50 on the 4, and $55 on the pass-line point 9, for a loss of $185.

Net Win: $136

Aggressive Approach - Single Odds Conclusion

Again, the Aggressive Approach and its method is not writ in stone. You can alter it to suit your game. For example, after each two repeats, you can simply go up two or three units and leave it at that, increasing every time you repeat two numbers by either two or three units.

Or you can increase your underlying bet by one-unit after each two repeats, if that more careful approach works for you. Or you can increase each underlying bet by one-unit after each and every repeat. Practice these methods and come up with the one that's best for you. The important thing to remember is that you're not giving up more than 0.8%, and with a hot roll full of repeating numbers, you stand to make a small fortune.

8. Double Odds - Aggressive Approach

With double free-odds allowed, everytime we increase our original or underlying wager, we're doubling up on our free-odds bet for that particular bet. For example, if we had $10 as our original wager, we'd be permitted to make a $20 free-odds bet. But if we increase our original bet to $15, then we go to $30 on our free-odds wager. Each increasing underlying bet causes double that to be made as a free odds-bet. With that in mind, let's examine a good solid aggressive approach using double odds.

The Betting Method

1. We make a pass-line bet of two units. As discussed before, it doesn't matter what units you use. You may be comfortable with $1 units or $5 or $25 or bigger units. It's all the same, just be sure you can afford to make these wagers financially or emotionally. Craps is a fast game, and money is won and lost fast. Be in control at all times.

After the point is established, we make a behind the line free-odds bet of four units.

2. We make a Come bet of two units, and back it up with four units as a free-odds wager.

3. We make another Come bet of two units, and again hand four units to the dealer as a free-odds bet.

4. We make yet another Come wager, our third, trying to establish three Come points. As soon as we do, with double odds, we stop betting and wait to see what happens.

5. If two Come or pass-line points or any combination of both repeat, we increase our wager by one additional unit and take double odds on it.

6. Thereafter, with two more Come or pass-line point repeats, we again increase our bet by one-unit.

7. After there have been four repeats, we increase our next bet by one more unit for every repeat that shows up, no matter how many there are.

Thus, we do the following:
• Increase our original bet by one unit after two repeats of points.
• Increase our original bet by one unit after another two repeats.

• Thereafter, we increase our original bet by one unit on every subsequent repeat. Let's follow a roll to see just how this is accomplished.

Sample Shoot: Aggressive Double Odds

We start with a $10 bet on the pass-line. The point is 4. We put $20 behind the line and make a $10 Come bet. The next *roll is a 5*. We give the dealer $20 as a free-odds bet at 3-2. We make a second Come wager and the *number thrown is 8*. We give the dealer an additional $20, and make a third Come wager of $10. The *next roll is a 10*. We again hand over $20 to the dealer as a double free-odds wager at 2-1 on the 10.

Now we wait to see what happens. We've covered three Come numbers, the 5, 8 and 10. We also have the 4 as a pass-line point. We've put down $40 in original bets and backed it up with $80 in odds bets, all double the original wager. The house has only 0.6% of an advantage, but we're most vulnerable at this point, with all that money out and a 7 as a possible killer.

The shooter shakes the dice and *rolls a 5*. Ok! We win our first Come bet, and collect $40.

Total Win: $40

We now have to make another Come wager in order to keep three Come numbers working for us. So we put out $10 and the shooter *rolls an 8*. Another winner. Our bet is *off and on*, and we collect $34.

Total Win: $74

We now have $10 in the Come box, but increase it to $15, because two points have been repeated. The *next roll is a 3*. We lose our Come bet.
Total Win: $59

We put out $15 (three $5 units) and the *shooter rolls a 6*. We give the dealer $30 as a free-odds bet at 6-5. We now have the 6, 8 and 10 as Come bets and the 4 as our pass-line wagers. We yell *even numbers*, for any point number that comes up even or as a pair wins for us. We're tempted to make hardways bets, for the dealer is imploring us to *bring out those even numbers with hardways*.

But we know better than to do this and give the house it's 9.09% or 11.1% on these dumb wagers.

The shooter rolls a 6 again. We collect $15 for our original bet and $36 for our odds wager.
Total Win: $110

We make another $15 wager in the Come box and the *shooter rolls a 4*. Another winner! We collect $50 for that bet, and now bet $20 on the pass-line, as the shooter prepares to come-out again.
Total Win: $160

The shooter rolls a 5. We back up our point with $40. So far the shooter has repeated points three times. One more and we increase our bet to $25. We have the 4, 8 and 10 as our Come numbers, and the 5 as our pass-line point. So we don't have to make any wagers. *The shooter rolls an 8*. We collect $10 + $24 for $34.
Total Win: $194

That was the fourth number repeated. We now make a $25 in the Come box, and the *shooter rolls a 9*. We back it up with $50. Now, for every repeated number, we increase our original bet by $5 or one-unit.

This is an aggressive way to play. At times we'll have a lot of money on the layout at risk, but if numbers repeat, we'll take in a ton of money. We end the theoretical roll here, having shown how an aggressive roll can make us money.

9. 10 Times Odds - Aggressive Betting Method

With 10 times odds, if the dice keep rolling, the cash will pour in as if we're minting money. But at the same time, with ten times odds, we can have a lot of money out on the layout.

Although ten times odds is offered at some Las Vegas casinos, we suggest not starting with $5 chips unless you can afford to take some hefty losses in the course of play. We'd suggest starting with $2 or $3 and doing the following. Let's start with a $2 bet.

1. Bet $2 on the pass-line and after the point is established, take ten times odds.

2. Make a Come bet and take ten times odds.

3. Make another Come bet and take ten times odds.

4. After you establish your last Come point, having bet $2 and taken $20 in free-odds, stop betting.

5. After every two repeats of point or Come numbers, increase your original bet by one unit or $1. Each dollar added requires $10 in additional odds. Stick with this method of increasing your bets by one unit for each two repeats. To get even more aggressive, after four repeats, increase your bets by one unit each time there's a repeat.

However, always be aware that you'll have a lot of

money out on the table at any one time. So don't just increase bets with hunches. Don't go against the dice. If the dice are hot and numbers are repeating, you'll see that in the money you take in and the increase in your bets. Go with the dice, not against them.

With ten times odds, a small fortune can be made in a quick period of time - if the dice go your way, so play it carefully, and increase your bets slowly as the dice repeat numbers. That's the sanest approach betting ten times odds.

Super-Aggressive Approach

The betting methods in this and the subsequent section are for those players who go for the jugular against the casino. When the hot roll comes, they want to have most or all of those numbers covered, so, as they repeat, they're constantly raking in the profits. But with this aggressive stance comes the likelihood of greater risk. Both have to be balanced. With that in mind, let's move to the single-odds game.

10. Single Odds - Super Aggressive

1. We start with a pass-line wager of three units. Three units gives us the chance to bet four units as a free-odds wager if the point is a 5 or 9, and five units if the point is a 6 or 8.

2. We then make a Come bet, taking maximum odds after putting down three units in the Come box.

3. We make another Come wager of three units and again take maximum odds.

4. If both the 6 and 8 are covered as Come bets or a combination of Come and pass-line bets, we make another Come bet of three units and again take maximum odds.

5. If only one of the numbers, 6 and 8, is covered after our two come bets, we make a place bet on the uncovered number (either 6 or 8) of six units. Thus, if we're betting with $1 chips, we put out $6 as a place wager. If we've been betting with $5 chips, we put out $30 and if we've been gambling with $25 chips, we have to lay out $150 as our place bet. All of these wagers, if the place number repeats, will be paid off at 7-6. We give the house 1.52%, the most we give away to the casino as its' advantage in any of our betting methods.

When we've established a pass-line wager and two Come wagers, one of them the 6 or 8, and a place number bet on either the 6 or 8, we've got the heart of the hot roll covered, namely, both the 6 and 8. Thus we have three numbers covered as pass-line and Come numbers, and one covered as a place number. We stop betting at this moment, and wait to see what happens.

Now, every time a number comes up, we add one unit to our underlying bet. Suppose the pass-line repeats. We add one unit to the pass-line wager. But suppose that the place number repeats. Assume it's a 6 and it repeats immediately. We add $12 to it if we've started with $30. If we've bet $150 in quarter chips, we add another $60 to it. If we've been betting $6, and we can get paid off at $3.50 to $3, we add $3. If not, we add $6.

There's another interesting thing that can happen. Let's assume that the pass-line point had been a 5, and it repeated. Or a come number repeated that was a 5. On the next roll, we have to make either a pass-line wager or a Come wager, whichever had repeated. Suppose this number is a 6, which is our place number. What we do is take down the place number and leave the 6 as either a pass-line or Come bet with free odds. That's always preferable to our place number. When that happens, we have only three numbers working, so we have to make another Come bet, to establish another working number.

If that number turns out to be any number not covered, we have our four numbers covered and stop betting.

6. We mentioned before that if the 6 and 8 are covered, we make another Come bet. By covered, we mean the 6 and 8 have either been pass-line or Come numbers, so we make another Come bet to get our four numbers covered. That's always our goal. Then, with each repeat, we raise the original bet by one unit, and keep doing this till the shooter sevens out.

7. If neither the 6 nor the 8 are covered as pass line or Come points, but three other numbers have been established, in that situation, we place six units on the 6 and 8 as place numbers. Now we have five numbers covered, the most we'll have covered in our betting method.

Should a pass-line or Come number repeat, we increase our bets by one unit. Should the pass-line or Come number rolled be a 6 or 8, we replace the 6 or 8 and make it a pass-line or Come number. If the 6 or 8 was repeated as a place number, we increase it by three units at a time after each repeat.

That covers all situations.

Super Aggressive Single Odds Summary
• If both the 6 and 8 are covered as Come or pass-line points, we make another Come bet, trying to get four numbers established.
• If only one, the 6 or 8 is covered by pass-line or Come rolls, we cover it as a place number with six units.

• If neither the 6 nor the 8 is covered as a pass-line or Come point, we cover both as place numbers with six units.

• When a Come or pass-line point is repeated, we increase the underlying bet by one unit. If the 6 or 8 is repeated as a place number, we increase it by $12 if betting $5 units, and when betting $25 chips, it is increased by $60.

That takes care of the single-odds Super Aggressive Approach. We want the 6 and 8 in this betting method, for they're theoretically the numbers most often repeated, and are usually the heart of any hot roll. To make certain that we have them, we have to give up 1.52% when they're place numbers.

11. Double Odds - Super Aggressive

1. We start with a pass-line wager of two units. It doesn't matter what the two units are - $1, $5, $25 or $100. Once the point is established, we make a maximum double odds bet behind the line.

2. We then make a Come bet, taking maximum odds after placing two betting units in the Come box.

3. We make another Come wager of two units and again take maximum odds. At this moment, we have two Come numbers as well as the pass-line wager working.

4. If neither the 6 nor 8 are covered, we now cover them both as place numbers, putting up six units on each. Then we stop betting. Thus we have three or four numbers plus the pass-line number working, depending on how many place bets we had to make.

If a Come number repeats now, we make another Come bet. If one of the place numbers, the 6 or 8 is our new Come point, we replace the place number and make it a Come number. Having two Come bets out plus a place number working, again we stop betting. If another Come number is taken down, we make another Come bet, this time increasing our bet by one-unit, for two numbers have repeated.

If the other place number is now rolled, we take the place number down, and keep it as a Come number. At this time, we have three Come bets working, plus a pass line number. And most importantly, we have the 6 and 8 covered almost from the beginning. That's the purpose of the Super-Aggressive Approach, to keep those numbers covered.

For every two repeats from now on, we increase the Come and pass-line wagers by one-unit. If a place number is involved, we increase it by $12 if it's $30, and by $60 if it's $150.

What can happen is that a repeat might affect the 6 or 8 as a Come number. If it is taken down, we replace it as a place number and stop betting. Thus, we'll always have four numbers alive for us - the pass-line, the Comes and the place number. This kind of switching back and forth may occur as numbers repeat, particularly the 6 and 8, which are always working after being established. This gives us a great chance of making a lot of money during the hot roll.

For every two repeats of a place number, increase it by $12 if betting $5, and by $60 if betting $25 chips. If betting $1, and you can paid at $3.50-$3.00, increase it by $3. If not, increase it by $6.

5. If after making two Come bets, we have only the 6 or 8 covered, we cover the other as a place number and stop betting. Then, if it comes up as a Come number later on, we replace it as a Come bet. This will happen after any Come number is repeated, and we make another bet to reestablish three working numbers besides the pass-line point.

We also increase our bets as mentioned before. After every two repeats, we increase the Come or pass-line bet by one-unit, and we increase the place bet by $12 if betting $5, by $60 if betting $25 and by $3 if betting $1 chips.

6. If both the 6 and 8 are covered after two Come bets have been made, we make another Come wager. We want to establish three points besides the pass-line point. If the next roll establishes our third Come point, we stop betting. Then after a repeat, we make another bet, either pass-line or Come.

12. Double Odds - Maximizing Super Aggressive

After two repeats, we increase our bets by one-unit and continue to do this after every two repeats from then on. After four repeats, you may want to go for it all, and increase your Come bets by one unit after each further repeat. If increasing the place numbers, do it also after each repeat, but only after four repeats have occurred. You may find this hot roll really taking off, and you want to gather in all the marbles.

One final note: If a pass-line point is repeated, and then the shooter rolls a 7 on his new come-out, all the Come bets will be taken down and lost, but not the free odds, which will be returned to you. But any place bets will remain, since they don't work on the come-out. Keep them, in place, and continue to make Come bets, trying to establish those three numbers besides the pass-line point.

13. Ten Times Odds - Super Aggressive

With ten times odds, we never make a place bet. The odds are too enticing, and the house advantage too low to even give them their 1.52%.

1. We make a pass-line wager of whatever is comfortable for you, whether it be $1, $2, $3, $5, $25 or more, then take ten times odds after the point is established.

2. We make an identical Come wager and again take ten times odds.

3. We make a second Come wager with ten times odds.

4. We make a third Come wager with ten times odds. Then we stop betting. We have four numbers working for us; three Come points and the pass-line point.

5. After two repeats, we raise our underlying bet by one unit and make a ten-times odds bet along with it.

That's this Super Aggressive Approach in a nutshell. We have three Come numbers instead of two working, and we increase our wagers by one unit after two repeats and each two thereafter.

If you really want it to get hairy, go for it all by increasing the betting unit by one after four repeats, and then one more after each subsequent repeat. If the dice keep repeating, you'll feel like you stumbled into the mint at Fort Knox, and people are throwing gold bars at you.

14. WINNING STRATEGIES: BETTING WRONG

Introduction

Money can be made in several ways at the craps table. One doesn't have to bet with the dice to win; fortunes have been won the other way by wrong bettors who wagered that the dice would lose. Among these players was the legendary "Nick the Greek," a wrong bettor all his life. He made and lost fortunes at the craps table, but some of his wins were stupendous. Why can't yours be stupendous also?

Anyone who plays casino craps gets a feel for a particular table. Some tables are hot, with numbers repeating all the time, with shooters making big and small scores. Yet other tables have an altogether different feel - at these tables, the dice are, to quote a long-time associate *as cold as a witch's teat, and you know how cold that is.* I don't know personally, but I'll take his word on that.

The main thing is that these cold tables are gold mines for wrong bettors. How can you tell if a table will be hot or cold. I wish I had the answer to that, for then I'd know the future. But I do know and you will, whether a table has been hot or cold. The hot tables have tons of action, with the gamblers screaming for numbers, with the bets so hot and heavy, they look as if they were shovelled on the green felt.

The cold tables have an eerie, empty feeling. The players here are moaning and groaning, for 90% of them will be betting with the dice and getting hurt. There will be spaces for new players. The stickman will be intoning his pleas in a tired voice, begging someone to break the mood, to get those dice burning again. If you're a wrong bettor, that's where you will want to be. So, let's slip in to that empty space next to the guy moaning that no shooter has made a point the whole table around. The dice are passed to us, but we decline them. We don't bet against our shoot. They move to the player to our left and we get ready to make our first bet.

CONSERVATIVE APPROACH
14. Single Odds - Conservative Approach

Since we're laying the odds, we don't necessarily have to search for a double odds game. Single odds can suit us just as well. Our goal is to get past the come-out and see numbers established. Each number out there switches the odds in our favor. We fear the come-out, because the shooter has twice as many chances (8) to get an immediate win as a loss (4), and only three out of those four losing rolls will help us, since either the 2 or 12 will be barred to us. So we want the shooter to roll a few numbers and then seven-out. That's serendipity to us.

1. We make a two-unit bet on don't pass. If a point is established, we now lay odds. Let's say we're betting with $5 chips. The shooter comes-out and rolls a 6. We now bet $12 to $10 against the 6. We place the odds bet next to our original wager and bridge the two bets with two $1 chips. Or we can simply place the odds bet next to the original wager and tilt the chips slightly. If the dealer wants to bridge the bets, let him do it.

2. We make a Don't Come wager of two units, and again lay odds. If the point is a 5 or 9, we lay $15-$10; if the point

is 4 or 10, we lay $20 -$10.

3. We make a second Don't Come bet of two units, or $10. Again, after another point is established, we lay the correct single odds.

Our goal is to establish two Don't Come points in addition to the don't pass point. Then we stop betting. Why do we stop? The more numbers out there, the more chances of those numbers repeating during a hot roll. We are content in this conservative approach to take in money bit by bit, or if lucky, in one fell swoop. For example, if the shooter now sevens-out, while all the other players will be moaning and giving us dirty looks, we're collecting $20 for our don't pass wager, $20 for each of our Don't Come bets, for a quick profit of $60.

4. Once the shooter sevens-out, increase the don't pass and subsequent Don't Come bets by one unit and lay the correct single odds.

Let's assume that the next shooter establishes a don't pass point for us. It's a 4. When betting wrong we like to see those outside numbers that are hardest to make. Now he rolls an 8. We've put $15 on the Don't Pass and $30 behind, and on the 8 we've put $15 and $18 as a free odds bet ($18-$15 or 6-5.) We make our second Don't Come wager and the shooter sevens-out. We lose the Don't Come wager of $15, but collect $30 and $30 for a $45 profit. The dice are still acting cold. We now bet $20 on don't pass.

Let's say the shooter now rolls a 7, and we lose the don't pass bet. Not to worry. We make another $20 bet. If that's lost by another 7, we reduce our don't pass wager to two units again.

5. Anytime two 7s come up (or a 7 and 11) on the come-out and we have more than two units bet there, we reduce to two units again. Anytime a shooter makes his pass-line point twice, or a combination of pass-line point and 7 or 11, we reduce our bet to two units. We don't fight the dice.

6. Another situation that may come up: The shooter comes-out with a 5 as his point. We had bet two units, and now lay three at 3-2. We make a Don't Come wager of two units. He throws a 9. We put three units as our free-odds bet. The original bet and the free-odds wager will be taken away by the dealer and put in the small space above the 9 place box, to designate a Don't Come wager.

We make another $10 bet in the Don't Come box and the shooter rolls an 8. We give the dealer $12 as our free-odds bet, and now stop betting. We have established two Don't Come points and one don't pass point. All we want is the magic 7 to appear and collect all our bets as winning ones.

But the shooter isn't listening to our silent plea. He rolls an 8, and we lose the Don't Come wager. We make another two-unit Don't Come bet, and he shoots a 6. We lay $12 against it, and right away the 6 repeats and we lose that bet.

7. Anytime one Come bet is repeated, we make one more. If another Come bet is then made by the shooter, we stop betting Don't Come till the end of his shoot. We only make another bet, this time on the don't pass, if he also makes his pass-line point. But we wait for his shoot to end without making any other Don't Come wagers.

Why do we do this? To protect ourselves against a monumental hot roll where he keeps knocking down our Don't Come bets and free-odds. It can get very expensive.

Once he seems to hold hot dice, we let the shooter run his course.

If the shooter again makes his pass-line point, we again make a don't pass wager of two-units. And then we lay the correct single odds and stop betting. We don't fight the dice. We wait patiently for the shooter to end his roll. By doing this at a table, I lost a few don't pass bets, but didn't get killed by the forty minutes the shooter held the dice and made point after point, murdering a couple of Don't Come bettors who stubbornly kept not only making their bets but increasing them, double suicide.

Don't fight the dice!!!

In that situation, you might ask - why didn't you switch and bet with the dice? I didn't because I've found in many years experience in the game that once you start switching around, you get whipsawed more often than not. You switch from the Don't to the pass-line and now the shooter sevens-out quickly. Or you switch from pass-line to don't pass, and he goes on an hours' tear with the dice.

You have to go to the table with one approach and stick to it. If you don't like what's happening at the table, you're not chained there. Go to another table. Or take a breather. But going back and forth from pass to don't pass leads only to regrets.

15. Double Odds - Conservative Approach

The difference between laying single or double odds is only 0.2%, changing the house edge from 0.8% down to 0.6%. When betting right, and you're taking odds, you're getting bigger payouts and a smaller casino edge. With double odds, laying them instead, you're getting the same thing, but risking a lot more. You're always putting more on the layout than you're receiving back if the dice go your way.

1. Make a two-unit wager, and after the point is established, lay double odds.

2. Make a Don't Come wager and lay double odds.

3. Make another, second Don't Come wager and again lay double odds. Stop betting.

4. If a Don't Come point is repeated by the shooter, make one more Don't Come bet, again with double odds. If another Don't Come number is repeated, stop betting to the end of the roll, until the shooter sevens-out or makes his pass-line point.

5. If he's made his pass-line point, then make another don't pass wager and lay double odds, but make no further bets. If his roll comes to an end, either by sevening-out or making his point, make another two-unit wager on don't pass. If he's made his point, don't make any other wagers. If he's sevened-out, make Don't Come wagers till you've established two Don't Come points.

6. If a shooter sevens-out without making a point, or only makes one Don't Come point, then increase your don't pass bet by one unit, and increase all Don't Come bets by one unit. So long as the shooter sevens-out and the dice move around the table, keep increasing that bet by one unit.

7. But once a new shooter makes a 7 twice in a row, or a 7 and 11, or two 11s, reduce your don't pass bet down to two units. Do this also if the shooter makes two pass-line points in a row. And then don't make any other wagers on Don't Come till the shooter sevens-out.

Double odds out on the table leaves you naked for awhile, when you've established all three points; the don't pass and the two Don't Comes. What you want is the 7 to show. It shows a lot more than any of the other numbers, and with a minimum edge to the house, you can make some good scores. But don't go against the dice. That's why we have these safeguards of reducing the don't pass wager and not making Don't Come bets after the shooter starts to make those dice hit numbers.

16. Ten Times Odds - Conservative Approach #1

Betting ten times odds on each point the shooter has to make puts a lot of money out on the table. But there's a good side to this. First of all, you can win quite a bit of cash if the dice run cold. And you have a minimum bet to be lost if the shooter rolls his 7 or 11 on the come-out. Once the point is established, the bulk of your bet is out. You'll sink or swim on the points, whether made or not made.

1. Make a one-unit wager if it's $5 or $25. If you're betting $1, then bet what you feel comfortable with, whether it's $1-$4. After the point is established, lay the ten times odds.

Ten times odds forces you to make some really big free-odds wagers. For instance, if you bet $5 on the don't pass and the point is a 4 or 10, you'd have to lay $100 to win $50. That's a big outlay.

2. Make a Don't Come wager of the same amount, and then lay ten times odds again.

3. Make another Don't Come wager and again lay ten times odds, then stop betting. If any number repeats, either a pass-line point or Come point, then make one more bet, lay ten times odds, and stop betting till the shooter sevens-out.

4. If the dice run cold and the shooter keeps sevening-out, then increase your original bet slightly. If betting $5, then make the underlying bet $7. The ten times odds situation will allow you to put plenty of money out on the table in any case. For example, if the point is a 4 or 10, now you're laying $140-$70. If it's a 5 or 9, you can lay $105-$70.

17. Ten Times Odds - Conservative ApproacH #2

Let's look at another method of betting at the ten times odds table, when going against the dice. Instead of raising the original wager, raise the odds you're laying. Here's how this would work.

Start by laying five times odds. If you keep winning, go to seven times odds, and then top out at ten times odds, as the dice keep getting cold. Then, if they're still cold, raise your original wager slightly, as recommended above. This would be - $2 at a time with a $5 wager, $10 at a time with a $25 wager, and $1 at a time with a $1 wager.

AGGRESSIVE APPROACH
18. Single Odds - Aggressive Approach

1. Make a two-unit wager, then lay the maximum free-odds. After the pass-line point is established, you make a Don't Come wager.

2. After establishing a Don't Come wager, lay the maximum free odds.

3. Make a second Don't Come wager and again lay the odds.

4. Make a third Don't Come wager, again laying the odds. Then stop betting.

Your goal is to cover four numbers, and hope for the 7 coming up fast. However, if a Don't Come or Don't pass-line point repeats, make one other bet, either on the Don't pass-line or Don't Come and again wait. Make no other wagers till the shooter sevens-out, or makes his point.

If he makes his pass-line point, let the roll go to the end without making any more wagers. Even if you wait twenty minutes, don't bet. When he sevens-out finally, start the cycle all over again.

5. If the dice are cold, raise your original bets by one-unit after each seven-out, and keep going like this, still trying to cover four numbers with single odds.

With this method, we have one extra number covered, and we're more aggressive in increasing our original bets so that if the dice stay cold for a long time we'll pick up some nice money.

The odds are working on Don't Come bets, even on the come-out, and sometimes you'll find yourself making two or three Don't Come bets, establishing the points, then the shooter makes his pass-line point. You lose that bet, and make another don't pass wager, but the shooter throws a 7. You lose the small don't pass bet, but all three of your Don't Come wagers are winners for you. Now, with a new cycle, you start all over again, and have no numbers up for the shooter to knock down by repeats.

The good thing about betting wrong is that the shooter must repeat a number for you to lose. If he can't repeat numbers, but throws up a bunch of points, and then sevens-out, you're going to have a field day.

19. Double Odds - Aggressive Approach

With double odds, we pretty much follow the same procedure as we did for the single odds Aggressive Approach.

1. We make a two-unit wager and lay double odds on the point. After making this don't pass bet, we now make a Don't Come wager.

2. After the first Don't Come point is established, we lay the double odds.

3. We make a second Don't Come wager, and again lay double odds.

4. We make a third Don't Come wager and again lay double odds. We want to have four numbers covered. Then we stop betting.

5. If a number repeats, whether a Don't Pass-line point or Don't Come point, we make no more bets and lay double odds. If that repeats, we stop betting and wait to the end of the roll.

6. If the dice are cold, we increase our wagers by one unit as original bets, and lay double odds on all don't pass and Don't Come wagers. But if two numbers repeat, we stop betting. When the roll ends by the shooter sevening out, we go back to our original wager of two units if he'd decimated all our numbers.

The dice may start to get hot, and we wait to see what happens. We don't anticipate what the dice will do; we know what they're doing from our betting patterns, which get bigger when the dice are cold, and smaller when the dice are hot.

Often, at a cold table, you're going to find the following pattern developing. You make a don't pass wager, and the point is 4. You had bet two-units or $10, and now lay $40-$20 as double odds.

You now make a Don't Come wager of $10, and the next throw is a 5. So you lay $30-$20 as a free-odds wager. Again you put $10 in the Don't Come box, but the shooter sevens-out. So you lose the $10 but win $60 for a net profit of $50.

Now you bet $15 in the don't pass box, and the point is 10. You lay $60-$30 as a double free-odds wager. You make a Don't Come bet and the shooter rolls a 5. Since you had bet $15, you now lay $45-$30 against the 5, and place another $15 in the Don't Come box. The shooter sevens-out. Net profit on this roll is $75. Total net profit so far is $125.

You now bet $20 in the don't pass box and the shooter rolls a 6. You now lay $48-$40 against the 6, and place $20 in the Don't Come box. The shooter rolls a 7. Net profit, $40, for a total profit of $165.

With a cold table, that's how the dice run. A couple of numbers are established, then the 7 shows.

If you want to play a little less aggressively, then increase your basic bet after every two seven-outs, instead of every one. It's more gradual, you stand less of a risk, and you can still make some good profits.

General Guidelines

Remember, all of these systems and methods are general guides, to show you how to bet intelligently and win some good money. But you can be flexible, and change them to suit yourself, either financially or emotionally.

The important thing is not to play hunches, to stay off shooters because you "have that feeling." Unless you're clairvoyant, don't do it. And don't keep switching sides. You'll give a bad whiplash to your bankroll.

20. Ten Times Odds - Aggressive Approach

With ten times odds, we again have that spectre of all that money out on the table at once. What you want to do with ten times odds in a nutshell is this. Establish three numbers, two as Don't Comes and one as a don't pass point.

Increase your basic bet by going from $5 to $7 then to $10 only if the shooter keeps sevening out. If betting $25, go from $25 to $35 to $50. If betting $1-$4, go up by one-unit, then two-units, then one-unit, then two-units. The same is true with the other bets. After going from $5 to $7 to $10 as your original bet, increase it to $12 if the dice keep running cold, and then to $15. It's a 2-3 upmove.

If the shooter makes one repeat, make another bet, but after the second repeat of a point, stop betting till the shooter sevens-out.

Be careful out there with the ten times odds. If things go your way, you'll drown in cash, but if they go against you, take the precautions we have recommended. Stay out of the roll, if the shooter keeps repeating numbers. Don't fight the dice. We can't repeat this often enough.

SUPER AGGRESSIVE METHOD

With the Super Aggressive approach, we keep making Don't Come bets and try to establish as many as possible.

21. Single Odds - Super Aggressive Approach

1. We bet don't pass with two units, and then, once the point is established, bet single odds against the point.

2. We make a Don't Come wager of two-units and again lay the single odds.

3. We keep making Don't Come wagers and laying odds till a number is repeated. Once the number is repeated, whether it be a pass-line or Come point, we make one more wager, and then continue to make Don't Come bets until another number is repeated. Once that second number is

repeated, we stop betting altogether until the shooter sevens-out.

4. If the dice remain cold and the shooter keeps rolling the 7 and winning for us, we increase our basic unit bet by one unit, going from two to three units, and then moving to four and five and so forth.

To play a little more conservatively, we can increase our betting unit after each two times the shooter sevens-out. But the main thing with betting super-aggressively is that we want to establish as many Don't Come bets as possible, so that if a 7 is rolled, we have several winners, all at single-odds.

With single-odds we don't have that much money out on the table, and we can bet more aggressively in raising our bets after each 7 ends a shooter's roll. But it's up to you to determine if you're comfortable with this method.

Practice it at home and see how it works for you. Just draw up a makeshift layout, showing the don't pass, the Don't Come box, and the place numbers. Use chips or coins and a pair of dice, and see how it all works out. If you're comfortable with it, it's a great system.

22. Double Odds - Super Aggressive Approach

1. We make a don't pass bet of two units and then lay double odds on the point established.

2. We then make continuous Don't Come wagers until we have all the numbers covered, or until a number is repeated by the shooter. Then we make another Don't Come wager, and after another repeat, if it happens, we stop betting.

Once we've established all the numbers, there's no point in making more Don't Come bets. You have to stop and see what happens. The same is true if you've established five numbers. You might stop then, or make that final Don't Come wager if there's a repeat.

The more numbers you establish, the more you can win if a 7 shows up on the dice. On the other hand, the more numbers you establish, the more targets you present for the shooter to knock down with repeating numbers. But what's on your side is this - he's got to repeat numbers. If he doesn't and sevens-out, you're going to make some good wins.

With double odds, we have double the money out that we have in the single-odds games. When increasing bets, you might want to be a little more careful and perhaps go up one unit at a time after every other come-out. But if you want to stay super-aggressive, then go up one unit after each seven-out.

23. Ten Times Odds · Super Aggressive Approach

Basically, you're doing the same thing you do with single and double-odds games. You make continuous bets trying to establish as many Don't Come points as possible. After one repeat, make one other bet. After two repeats, stop betting till the shooter sevens-out.

When the dice are cold and you're winning, there are two ways to approach a super aggressive stance. One, the more risky and more rewarding, is to take the full ten times odds, and increase the basic unit bet from $10 to $12 to $15 after each 7 out. Use the same proportions when betting more or less than $5 chips.

The other method is to start with only five times odds,

and with each seven-out, increase the odds by one or two at a time. Thus, after a shooter sevens-out, you go to six times odds and then seven, then all the way to ten.

If the dice are still cold, now you can increase your basic bet as shown above. We used $10 as a basic bet. If that's too big for you, since you're laying from five to ten times odds, you might start with $5. Or you might go with $1-$4. It's up to your bankroll, and your inclination to take risks in the hope of getting big rewards.

Practice at home and try the various methods. See what suits you best. If you can make money at home in practice, and feel comfortable with the betting arrangement and the sums involved, then you might try it under actual casino conditions.

15. BETTING LIMITS

Minimum Bets

I guess there are still places in the smaller towns of Nevada, and in the downtown joints of places like Reno and Las Vegas, where you can still play craps for a 25¢ minimum bet. The games attract a ragtag of gamblers, locals down on their luck who never had any luck but bad luck, transients waiting to raise money for the next bus out of town, and so forth.

You can still find $1 minimum games in all kinds of places in Nevada, but the Strip hotels in Las Vegas may eliminate or restrict them, especially on busy weekends or times when the casinos are packed, such as the week of a really big prizefight in Vegas. Then you're more apt to find $5 minimum games available. If $5 is too steep, go to one of the smaller casinos or casinos which cater to the smaller bettor. You shouldn't have trouble finding them.

So, unless you're in Atlantic City on any crowded night or weekend, you should find a $1 or $3 game, if that's the level of play you're comfortable with. In Atlantic City you might find minimum $5 tables in the more glamorous casinos, but you can walk the Boardwalk and possibly find a smaller game, such as a $2 or $3 minimum casino craps table.

Once you're comfortable at a $5 table, you'll find a number of these. However, in Atlantic City, when it's packed to the gills, the bosses open minimum $25 and $100 tables, and it might be hard to find a place at a $5 table. If there are none available, go to another casino. You'll eventually find a place for yourself at a table.

But don't go to a $25 minimum table just because it's the only spot in the casino where there's room for you. If you're a $5 player with a $5 player's bankroll, there's going to be too much pressure on you and your bankroll. It's better not to play than to take risks like that. Be sane when you gamble.

This book is not written to encourage the readers to run out and take their hard-earned bucks and gamble them away. Not at all. This book is written because too many people gamble badly, and throw their money away as a result. People love to gamble, and the statistics prove it. But why should the casinos get the money? Gamblers and players deserve their share.

Many people avoid craps, with it's low 0.6% house edge, and will play roulette, with it's 5.26% edge for the house, because they don't understand craps. After reading this book, they should understand the game as well as any casino executive. So, if people are going to a casino and want a chance to gamble and possibly make money, it's much wiser for them to be standing at the craps table than sitting at the roulette table. Or throwing away their coins at the slots, for that matter.

Maximum Limits

We've spoken about minimum limits. Finding big maximum limit games is no problem. Casinos will accommodate players to sky-high limits. That is, most casinos. There are casinos, whose bosses have a philosophy, "lets grind out the grinds." What they means is this - if they only allow small bets to be made, they can't get hurt, and their edge on the bets that are made will add up. They don't allow themselves to get hurt by a lucky run of dice for the players, because they keep their maximum bets low. Some will only allow $200; others $500 as a maximum bet.

However, the bigger casinos in AC and Vegas and other gambling centers have raised their limits substantially from what used to be $500 or $1,000 as a maximum bet on any area of the casino layout. If you are in the money and want to gamble big, the casinos will accommodate you. If you want to make a $5,000 bet in Atlantic City, you'll have no trouble. You can even make a bigger bet. It depends on the casino.

If you're that type of gambler, a premium player, a gambler who bets *really really* big, and wants to know what limits the house has, speak to the floorman before you start playing. He'll give you the parameters of play. He'll probably know who you are, because the big players don't come to the casinos with bagfuls of cash; they have extensive credit already established.

So, if you have a million dollar line at a casino in AC or Vegas, discuss just what bets you can make, and then if you want to, make them. No problem.

It's interesting that the casino with the biggest limit, as far as I know, is one that will also allow a player to bet $1 as a minimum bet at the tables. I'm talking about the Horseshoe Club in downtown Las Vegas. They'll cover practically any bet. On huge amounts, such as a million-dollar bet, it would probably require an ok from someone in the Binion family, the family that runs and owns the casino privately, but it may also come from someone with authority from the family.

I've seen small games suddenly transformed into megabucks games with the arrival of a high roller. Whereas there was a $100 total on the layout, suddenly there are $50,000 bets being made.

Casinos will sometimes also do something else for the *whale*, the term for the biggest of the big. It will give him a table to himself, and eliminate all other gamblers. So now the whale and his friend or friends can roll the dice all the time and make whatever bets they want, without being bothered by other players. They set their own pace at the game, without waiting for an old geezer who's arguing that he had a buck on the hard 4, but the stickman forgot to put it there and covered the hard 10 instead.

For most of the readers, who are not *grinds* or *whales*, the casinos will have limits that will easily accommodate your wagers at the table. But sometimes, you might find the dice going all your way, and with our sane increasing of bets when winning, you might now be making bets you thought you wouldn't make, in the hundreds of dollars. If in doubt as to the house limit, ask just what limit wagers you can make.

A Cool $22,000 Win

I was advising an older gentleman once, who bet quarters ($25) as his basic bet. His old method of betting was to make a pass-line wager, take single odds (no matter what odds were offered) and then put out $160 on all the place numbers. Then he'd wait patiently for the $160 to come back to him, and then he'd increase each place bet by $5. Even with a hot roll, he made a diddly-wink, and with cold rolls, the $160s were being scooped up by the dealers.

I changed his game, first by having him play in a double odds casino, and then eliminating the place numbers in favor of Come bets with double odds. He covered two

Come bets and then I told him to place the 6 or 8 if they weren't covered (he loved those numbers.)

This man had plenty of money in the bank, and he loved to play craps. The $25 level made no difference to him one way or another. He figured he'd lose so much for each visit to Vegas. If he got into some really hot games, he made a few thousand profit for the five days he spent in the gambling capital of America.

Now with his new game, when a hot roll came, he started to pile in the money. He would extend his Come bets to three and four, and always cover the 6 and 8. One night, a friend of his was shooting dice, another older gentleman who never bet more than $5 but also liked the game and was my student's neighbor in New Jersey. Well, this other guy held the dice for over an hour, and as the bets escalated, the boxman squirmed and the floormen, who treated the older gentleman as a pet, now saw him as a problem to their bankroll.

After fifty minutes, my student asked the question, "just what's the maximum limits?" That was a question he had never asked before. He was told they'd take bets up to $3,000. I think they would have taken higher bets, but they just pulled some arbitrary figure out of their hat.

The table was now packed, as word of the hot shoot spread, and chips poured down on the layout. My man kept increasing his wagers. When the shoot finally ended, he had to take a few racks with him loaded with casino checks, plus the many he had stuffed in his jacket pockets, all his pockets.

His profit was $22,000. He couldn't believe it. He had never won more than $4,500 at one time, and that was with the same kind of hot shooter. The house didn't have to worry about its' maximum limit, but the older guy said to me, "did you see their faces when I asked about the maximum limit?" he grinned and winked, and I think he got a bigger kick out of seeing the fear in the floorman's eyes, than in his nice win.

16. MONEY MANAGEMENT - ALVIN B'S STORY

Introduction

Money management is a key element in gambling of any kind, just as it is in life. Without managing your money correctly, the rent doesn't get paid, the mortgage is two months behind, the bills pile up. Without money management, even if you can can pay all your bills, you don't get a chance to save or to invest. There's nothing for a rainy day. Imagine how many millions of Americans live on plastic, the ubiquitous credit card, from one 19 1/2% interest payment to another. If they had correctly managed their money, if they had dined out less frequently or didn't buy those expensive personal gifts, if they had bought a $12,000 car instead of a $35,000 one - the list goes on and on.

I'm not preaching to anyone, believe me. But there's a certain peace of mind that comes with proper money management in life and in gambling, and there's also no real sense of regret when managing money correctly.

Often, with all other things being equal, money management is the difference between winning and losing.

ALVIN B'S STORY

I can think of a gambler I knew well. Let's call him Alvin B (not his real name.) He was a local in Vegas and had lived there for fifteen years. He had a comfortable living in real estate, while everything was going up and up, but when prices steadied, then dropped, when the book of listings of houses for sale the realtors used resembled the Manhattan telephone book, with thousands and thousands of listings, Alvins' income dropped off to nearly nothing.

He hadn't really managed his money wisely. He had a Mercedes, his wife had a smaller Mercedes, his daughter at college in the East had a BMW, and his son, who was trying to establish a career as an actor in Hollywood (good luck!!!) had a Jaguar convertible (his dream car!!!) to tool his talentless body around.

Alvin had a gold Rolex, his wife had all sorts of baubles. He had heavy debts from other ostentatious spending. Money in, money out. We were once discussing investments and Alvin confided that, other than 100 shares of IBM, and $5,000 in a CD, he had nothing else in ready assets.

At that moment, he had to pause to write out another check for his son, and one for payment of his daughter's BMW. Well, when the money stopped coming, there were arguments with his wife, who packed up and left him one day, and filed for divorce. Alvin wasn't doing so well.

Alvin occasionally played craps. That's how we had met, at the DI one evening, standing next to each other. I was living in Vegas at the time, and we went out to eat later on at a Japanese restaurant he knew. It was an expensive Sushi house, and for some tidbits, our bill came to $110. Amazing, the way he found places to throw his money away in.

He played a bad game of craps. He placed all the

numbers like a lot of other foolish craps players, and he compounded the injury by constantly pressing or doubling his bets. I told him at dinner that trees didn't grow to the sky - an old saying in the stock market. It was an analogy of his craps system, but he stared at me blankly, thoughtfully chewing on some sashimi.

"What I mean," I said, "if you keep doubling up like that, the 7 is going to come, and you have nothing to show for it. Wouldn't it be better to increase your bets more slowly and pocket money as the numbers repeat?"

"Hey, that's for the nerds," he said. "I'm always after the big score. I try to sell the million dollar house - let the nerds sell the $70,000 fixer uppers. I want the big commission." His gold Rolex glinted in the dim light of the restaurant.

As his house of cards collapsed around him, I saw him from time to time. Then we met again, once more at a craps table on the Strip, a new fancy place that catered to high rollers. Alvin had a credit line there, as he had in several other joints, and when I stood next to him, he was asking for another five thousand in credit.

"Alvin," I said softly. I was going to ask how he was doing, but I could see from the $100 or so chips in his rails, he was doing lousy. He signed a marker for the 5 large ones, and pushed the $100 checks tightly into the rail. Then he put three hundred on the pass-line, and the point was 6. He put another $300 behind the line.

"They allow double odds here, " I said.

"I hate the 6. I love the outside numbers. 6s are for nerds."

He gave the dealer $1,500 to place on all the remaining numbers, $300 on each. Then he rubbed his hands together and waited for the shoot to continue. I was to his left and the shooter was to his right. He was next in line for the dice.

The shooter tried. He talked to the dice, he shook them as if they were unruly mice, but all he could manage was a 3, a 2 and an 8. Then he sevened out.

"Goddamn nerd," came out of Alvin's mouth, as he gave the hapless shooter a dirty look. Now he had the dice. The tray containing all the dice was pushed to him and half a dozen dice spilled out. Alvin took a while to make his selection. Why the two he selected had any particular appeal to him, I don't know. But he was satisfied with the two red cubes, and now started emptying his rails. He had about $3,000 left, and put $500 on the pass-line.

He shook the dice. I didn't make a bet. I was caught up in his world of hurt and just watched. He rolled a 7.

"Yes," he yelled. "Yes!"

Then he turned to me as payoffs were made around the table. "I need a good shoot. I can't even cover the marker. Things have been terrible. Root for me."

"Alvin," I said, as he pressed his pass-line bet to $1,000. "Maybe leave it at $500. See what happens."

"This is my style," he said. "Don't tell me what to do, ok?"

"Sure."

He threw the dice. The point was an 8. To me, the best points when betting with the dice are the 6 and the 8, for each can be made in five ways. They are the heart of any hot roll. But to Alvin, the 6-5 odds held no interest. He didn't even make a free-odds wager.

He paused, as the dice were passed to him. Then he pulled out his chips, holding about $2,500 in the rails. He put $500 on the 5 and $500 on the 9. That left him $1,500. Then he put $750 on the 4 and 10. He didn't even buy those terrible numbers.

Now he had just about everything out on the table. His

rails held about $30 in $5 chips. Alvin took a deep breath and rolled the dice. He rolled a 4.

"Yes," he yelled, as $1,350 was slid over to him. He pushed the chips back to the dealer. "Make the 4 $1,500 and the rest on the 10. So now he had the 4 at $1,500 and the 10 at $1,350. It would have been wise to buy both these numbers and get a correct 2-1 payoff. If he had done this before the roll, his payout would have been $1,500 instead of $1,350. But there was no use talking to him.

"I've got a feeling", he shouted, " a wonderful feeling." He rolled the dice, and I could see a deuce on one. The other matched.

"Four," said the stickman.

"Yes, yes, yes." $2,700 in chips were shoved to Alvin. At this point, he could have kept the $2,700 and still have had all the numbers out there to get back the $1,800 he needed to get even.

But this wasn't his way. He made each of the outside numbers a beneficiary of the roll. The 5 and 9 were pressed up to $1,000 each. Then he put an additional $150 on the 10, to make it even with the 4 at $1,500. Now, I figured, he'd put away the remaining $1,650 into the rails. But instead he made the 4 and 10 $2,500 bets each.

He fingered the remaining two $25 chips. "What should I do with these?" he asked me.

"Keep them."

What a nerd!" he threw them to the stickman. Hard 4 and 10. Half and half with the boys." He was profusely thanked by the crew.

He shook the dice and rolled the 9. $1,400 more came his way. He looked down at the chips and around the table. Oh, no, I thought, not again. But once more Alvin sprang to action.

If he was really smart, he'd take it all down and make a $500 Come bet. That would give him a profit now of $3,400 less $500 or $2,900.

That's not bad for about fifteen minutes work. Or even less. Most of the delay was Alvin's doing, figuring out what to do with the chips on the table. He made the 4 and 10 $3,000 each. That took care of $1,000. With the remaining $400 he made the 5 and 9 $1,200 each.

He shook the dice violently. I was praying for him. Hoping he'd come to his senses, and take it all down now.

Or after he made another outside number. Anything but this insanity. He rolled a 3. It meant nothing to him, for he had nothing going at all in the Come box. Well, if he had made a Come bet that would have lost him $500. Now he rolled an 11. That would have evened him out. He rolled an 8 next, then another 8.

"Goddamn dice," he said to me, "they've turned bad."

"Then take it all down," I whispered.

"What?"

"Alvin, you know how much you have out there?"

"You're the numbers guy. How much?"

"Eighty four hundred dollars." I paused. "You pay off your marker and you're ahead $3,400."

"That's one marker. That's my second. I'm in for ten large ones."

"Jesus."

He shook the dice and sevened out.

Ashen faced, he abruptly left the table. He walked to a nearby bar and ordered a drink. The dice passed to me. I made a pass-line bet and held the dice for close to fifty minutes. If he had taken down the bets, or even reduced them in half, with his style of betting, Alvin would have easily picked up $60,000-$100,000. If, if, if.

His idea of managing money was to keep pressing it up, waiting for the axe to fall. The tree doesn't go to the sky. That's a good lesson for anything, even life.

Alvin no longer lives in Vegas. He's moved to Ridgewood, New Jersey, where I understand he's met a woman and shares a place with her. When I spoke to him last he told me he was managing a movie theatre in a mall nearby, waiting for another real estate boom. In the meantime, he's doing what he can. I asked him about Atlantic City.

"I go there once in a while. Play a little craps, but not the way I used to. I drag my bets now, take my profits and run. I learned my lesson."

I guess he has.

17. THE PLAYER'S BANKROLL

Introduction

There are two aspects involved in choosing a bankroll for playing. First of all, you must decide how much you're taking for your entire stay at the hotel casino. Secondly, you must figure out a bankroll for one complete session of play.

You can look at the situation from two sides. First of all, you can say, "I'm going to be playing right, with $10 as my first bet on the pass-line, and taking double-odds on all bets. And I'm going to play conservatively, but if I win serious money, I might move to a more aggressive stance." Ok, in that situation, you can figure out just how much you need if you're playing for the day, or for three days or for a week.

On the other hand, you can say to yourself, "I've got $5,000 set aside for gambling purposes. What should my betting limits be if I stay for one day at Atlantic City, or I'm playing there for two days, or I'm going to Vegas for four days or a week?"

Those are the two correct approaches. Some of you have various sums that you can set aside for gambling at your discretion. Others have a limited fund, and that limit will determine what stakes you'll play for.

Before we go any further, let's make one thing perfectly clear. You don't have to gamble. You don't have to play craps. But if it's your game and you want to play at a sane level, then read on. And never think of gambling at a casino if you can't afford to lose financially or emotionally. Don't play with money you can't afford to lose. Don't play with money that should go for necessities. Think of gambling money as expendable money that won't hurt you if you lose it. This is not to say you'll end up losing it, but if you can't make the rent or a mortgage payment if you lose the cash at the craps table, forget about gambling.

This the first way to get ready to gamble. The other will be with a fixed bankroll. If you decide to bet right, with the dice, and want to start with $5 bets, let's see how much you'll need for your complete bankroll. Let's always start with a conservative approach, and then work from there.

There's a lot of single-day action in Atlantic City, by gamblers who take the bus down or drive to the resort city by the ocean and play for one solid day, then return home the same evening. Since AC has single-odds craps, we'll study just how much money a player must have for the day's action. This discussion also holds true for the riverboats, Indian gambling, Nevada, or anywhere else you play single odds craps. We're also going to assume that the player will be at a $5 minimum table, for it's difficult to find anything less than that, especially on weekends or in the evening.

With that in mind, let's review our bets.

A. BETTING RIGHT
1. Single Odds

• **Single Session.** We should put out three units or $15 on the pass-line. That gives us the chance to bet four units on the 5 and 9 as free-odds bets and five units on the 6 and 8, also as free-odds bets. Playing most conservatively, let's assume that the pass-line point is a 6, and our two Come points are 8 and 9.

Our total expenditure before another roll of the dice is as follows: $15 + $25 on the 6, $15 + $25 on the 8 and $15 + $20 on the 9. That's a total of $115 or **23 units**, with the most conservative play possible under our betting methods. This gives you a chance to win big, and gives the house an edge of less than 0.8%, because of the extra free-odds on the 6, 8, 5 and 9.

We suggest that you have at least seven times your individual cycle stakes of 23 units, or about **160 units,** as your single session table bankroll. That comes to $800 using $5 units.

These 160 units will allow you to ride out some losing streaks, waiting for the good rolls that will make you some good money. It will give you an ample cushion in the course of play.

• **One Day's Play.** If you're down there for one day's play, just how many times will you play at a table? With several sessions worth of play, then take about **500 units** with you - almost 3 times the single session bankroll. If it's $5 units, take $2,500 with you, and if you're going to play $25 units, have $12,500 with you. That will be plenty for $5 and $25 games respectively, and will give you tons of action.

$1 unit bettors using the average three unit bets as we did with the $5 and $25 bets, should take $500.

Having this much with you doesn't mean you're going to lose it all. It just gives you the chance to win big, without resorting to **scared money**, which is inadequate funds forcing you to either take chances or avoid chances to win, both bad moves.

Again, we strongly suggest that you play our conservative approach and not play any wilder game. Don't make foolish bets on hardways; don't even give the casino it's 1.52% edge on the place numbers 6 and 8.

Once you start winning, you can play a more aggressive game. But only then. Remember, you're giving the house only an 80¢ theoretical win for every $100 you bet wagering our way. You'll be playing sanely.

Space out your play, and play less the first day, unless you're on an incredible winning streak. Then, by all means, go with the flow. But, if not, if you're winning or losing slightly, play a few times one day and a few times the next. Make your money count, and also leave yourself a clear head when you're at the table. Don't get exhausted and so tired, you forget to make bets and get all mixed up. Be relaxed everytime you're at the tables.

• **Fixed Bankroll - One Day's Play**. If you have $2,400 ready to gamble with, you can play the $5 tables about three or four times comfortably in one day. We're talking worst-case scenario, losing $500-$700 at a clip. This is a real longshot to happen. It probably won't happen. You'll have winning sessions and losing sessions, and the bankroll we suggest should carry you easily through the day.

• **Fixed Bankroll - Two Day's Play.** For a total two day bankroll, take four times a one session's stake for a total of **640 units**. And take our advice to curtail play the first day so that you're rested up for more action the second day. Stick with our formula for conservative bettors. You'll find it is a sane approach to the game.

If it's a $5 game, we'll take $3,200 or $3,000 to round it off; for a $1 game, take $640 - $600 will do; and for a $25 game, $16,000. It sounds like a lot of money, and it is a lot of money, but this is not to say you're going to lose it all. It just gives you that comfort zone and avoids a situation where you run out of money just as a hot shoot develops.

My theory about right betting is this - you take the small losses and wait for the big score. It's like a fight where you're the slugger. You're up against a boxer who's jabbing you and cutting you and hurting you, but you've got the good left hook and right cross, waiting to throw them in combination.

What usually happens at a craps table is this - you lose slightly and lose and lose slightly some more, then the hot roll comes and you get it all back plus plenty more in one fell swoop. That hot roll is going to be there - you want to make sure you're there with money when it develops. There's nothing worse than being tapped out just as the hot roll comes and the table comes alive with screaming and happy gamblers.

When we mention $16,000 we're assuming you're betting three units of $25 each. That's a big game. However, you might want to bet just $25 as your pass-line wager. In that case, you should have $5,000 for three to four plays in one day. For four to six plays, you should have about $6,500.

What we recommend is a gradual increase according to

how well you're doing. You can't ever anticipate what the dice are going to do. So you might start with the $15 bet we recommend, and then, if your bankroll improves by about $1,200, go to the single bet of $25 and move up from there as your bankroll improves. But it's a great jump from betting $15 to $75 on the pass-line. Unless you're adequately funded, don't even try to bet those limits.

If you're betting more modestly, trying the $3 pass-line bet, you'll need a bankroll that's proportionately less taxing. Making a pass-line wager and taking single odds, making two Come wagers with single odds will cost you an average $23. About seven times that, to round it off, would be $150.

If you take about $600 with you, or if your bankroll totals $600, forget about $5 games, and stick to the $1 tables where you start with a $3 bet. Or, if you can't find a $1 table available, go to the $5 table and make a single $5 wager on the pass-line. If you do this, your average bets on the pass-line, two Comes and Free-odds will be $30. Taking $200 to a table should be sufficient, and having about $750 for a day's play should do it for you.

As you see, you don't have to jump from $3 bets to $15 bets, or from $15 wagers to $75 bets. There are plenty of stops in between. If you start with $3 and do well, go to $5, then to $10 and finally to $15, if you want to be extra careful about your bankroll. And only move up if you're winning. Never increase bets when losing, chasing that elusive rainbow. You are flirting with trouble. Increase your bets as your bankroll expands; that's the wisest course we can recommend.

• **Single Odds - Extended Play.** By extended play, we mean anywhere from three days to a week - players staying for an entire weekend, or for the Sunday-Thursday spread, or for a full week. If they're playing a single-odds game, we recommend a total bankroll of **800 units** for extended play - a total of five times the single session bankroll.

Thus, if you're betting unit is $1, bring $800; if $5 bring $4,000; if $25, you'll need $20,000. For extended play, these padded bankrolls give you lots of leeway to take a small hit and bounce back on top. Don't forget, that while these figures may seem high, again, $25 bettors are putting out $575 on just one cycle of play.

A session is as long as it takes - there's no fixed amount. You might find yourself at a horrible table, and after losing about $500, have no confidence in the dice, so you leave. Wise decision. It might have taken twenty minutes. The next table is choppy - the dice pass, they don't, and after an hour and a half, you add everything up and find you're ahead $210. You leave.

The next table is moderately bad, and after an hour's play, you're down $300 but you're tired of the game and need a rest. So you leave. You've played your three sessions for the day, and ended up down $590. You've brought along $4,000. You're betting three units of $5 each, taking single odds and making two Come bets.

The second day starts off badly. It's another choppy table, and after being there close to two hours, all you have to show for it is a $140 loss. You take a break, put on your swimsuit, take a dip, look at the bikini beauties around the pool. You have lunch, take a nap, return to the tables about four in the afternoon.

You're relaxed and the dice here are fairly good. You're ahead about $700, when they turn cold, and before you give it all away, you leave with a $300 profit. That evening, you play for about an hour, and book a $350 loss. So, at the end of the second day, a day you lost $190, you're down $780. Your bankroll is still healthy, at $3,220.

A dinner, a show, a meeting at the bar. It's a nice evening, and with company, you decide not to return to the tables that night.

The next morning, you have a light breakfast of orange juice, cold cereal and toast, and a couple of cups of coffee. To the tables. You hit a buzzsaw. The dice are cold, ice-cold, and after a little over half an hour, you're down $700. You're gone, Your bankroll is now hovering at the $2,520 mark. You're still ok.

You decide to forego the afternoon game, and instead call up your woman from the night before, and relax all afternoon. After dinner, you give the tables another try.

You start with your $800 and lose about $350 of it before you get the dice. Then the numbers start rolling in tandem, and it's one point after another. From the conservative game, you start covering the 6s and 8s, for they're coming up every other roll. Your nickel chips become quarter chips and then move to $100 (dollar) chips. By the time you finish your roll, your rails are packed, as is one pocket of your jacket.

You leave the game right after you relinquish the dice and count up your winnings, $4,860. At this point you have a bankroll of $8,860. You've more than doubled your bankroll.

There's one more day to play, but you forego the AM game. You eat a big breakfast and relax around the pool all morning. That afternoon you walk the Strip and then meet your squeeze before dinner. It's dinner and a show for the two of you, and just before turning in, you go with her to the tables.

You can now play a bigger game, but you want to leave

a winner. You'll see what the dice will do. If they were hot the last time, maybe just one more hot run. You'll let the dice decide your fate - if they run well, you'll be increasing your bets. If not, you'll pack it in. Your plane leaves the next day at 10 AM.

So you go to the table, rested, relaxed, a winner. You start with your $15 bets and the dice are fairly good. You're up about four hundred bucks, and think, "hey, I doubled what I brought out here. Why go on?" So you cash in, take your babe to the room.

The next day you fly home. Beautiful trip. One big win did it all for you. You played sanely and conservatively till the dice got hot, then you started pumping in those bets, letting those chips speak for you.

But most importantly, though your bankroll was never in jeopardy, you had more than enough, you never truly worried about going broke. That's the pleasure of being adequately funded.

· Single Odds - Aggressive and Super Aggressive Play
Instead of 160 for each individual session, we suggest you bring 200 units to the table, whether playing Aggressive or Super Aggressive. Therefore, for a day's play, such as three full sessions, we suggest 600 units. For two days play, we suggest 800 units, and for extended play, 1,000 units.

A better approach, which we recommend, is to start conservatively, and if the dice start passing, move to an aggressive or super-aggressive stance. This can happen as the hot roll develops. But always be sure to move up slowly and sanely, so that you're taking profits off the table. In this way, when the dice seven-out, no matter what you have on the table, you have a solid profit already in the rails.

• **Betting Conservatively - Single Session**. If betting $1 chips, and betting *two units* instead of three as we did in our other examples, you will bet approximately $15 per series. You need $100 for the session conservatively, but we suggest $150 per session if betting aggressively or super aggressively. With a single $5 unit as your basic bet, you will be betting $30 per series, and need $300 for a super-aggressive or aggressive stance at the tables.

With three $25 chips as your basic bet each series is costing you about $525. If betting aggressively, count on each series costing you about $650, so multiply that by seven and you have $4,550 needed for a single session. You'll need about $13,000 per day to play. Just multiply the $4,550 by three for one day's play (as above), four times for two day's play, and five times for extended play.

Again, this is not to say that you'll use up your bankroll, but you want it to be solidly there for you in case you run into early losses.

2. Double Odds

Let's assume you're betting two-units of $5 each on the pass-line, taking double odds, and making two Come bets of two-units with double odds - six units per bet. That's a total of $90 out on the table, 18 units. Seven times 18 units is 136 units - let's say 130 to make it easier. If betting $5 units we suggest bringing about $650.

That's what you need for single-session play. If you play three times in the day, count on approximately $2,000 as your bankroll.

If you're more comfortable with $2 as your pass-line wager, then your three bets with double free odds comes to about $15 (counting $5 on the 6 and 8.) Multiply that by 7 and you have $105. You can play comfortably with $100.

For a day, count on $300-$400.

With $25 chips and betting three units, you need about $3,000 per session. It's a big game. Count on $10,000 for the day's work at the tables.

For extended play, again, give yourself five times a single session stake for the total bankroll, four times if you're playing for two days.

Why do we multiply by 7 for a single session? To give ourselves the benefit of a slow start, of ice cold dice at the outset. By multiplying by seven, we give ourselves a lot of leeway. We conserve our capital in the hope of getting that hot hot roll.

• Double Odds Aggressive and Super Aggressive Play

If betting $5 chips and betting three-units at a time, take $800 with you to a table, instead of the $650 for the more conservative game. Thus we want to bring 160 units for a single session. Have about $2,500 (500 units) ready for a full day's play, $3,200 (640 units) for two days, and $4,000 (800 units) for extended play. That will give you a big cushion as far as your bankroll is concerned.

Betting a single $25 chip require close to $1,800 for a single session of play. Count on about $5,400 for the full day.

These figures will more than adequately fund your bankroll.

If you're betting with $1 chips, and start with a $2 wager, be prepared to bet about $130 for each session of play. That's about $500 for a day, with an additional $400 for extended play. Again, that will more than cover you as far as your bankroll is concerned.

B. BETTING WRONG
1. Single Odds

• **Single Session - Conservative Play**. If betting $3 on the don't pass and making additional $3 bets on Don't Come, after three points, such as a 4, 5 and 6 are established, we'd lay out $9 as underlying bets, and $6 on the 4, $3 on the 5 and $6 on the 6 for a total of $24. If we multiply that by seven, we get a total of $168 for single-session play.

If betting $10 on the don't pass, and additional $10 wagers on two Don't Come points (4, 5 and 6) we lay out $30 as our underlying bets, and an additional $47 on the free-odds, for a total of $77. Multiplying that figure by seven gives us a total of $539. We can round it off to $550 for a single session of play.

If we bet a single $25 chip on the don't pass, and the same bet on the two Don't Comes, we have $75 as our underlying bets. Add to that $50 on the 4, $30 on the 5 and $30 on the 6, we get a total of $185 for a series of rolls. If we multiply that by seven, the total is $1,295. A bankroll of $1,200 should easily cover us.

• **Single Odds - Day and Extended Play**. Assuming we go to the craps table three times a day, we'd need $500 for a $3 game, $700 for a second day and $850 for extended play. With $5 units we'd need $1,500 for the day, $2,000 for a second day and $2,500 for extended play.

With a single $25 chip out, we'd need $3,600 for a day's play, $4,800 for a second day and $6,000 for extended play.

If we're betting three $25 chips as our basic bet, then multiply the preceding paragraph figures by three - about $10,000 for the day, $14,000 for a second day and about $18,000 for extended play.

Betting $75 at one time is involving yourself in a big game. Our best advice is to work your way up to that figure slowly and carefully. If you encounter a cold table, you can find your original $15 bets escalating up to $75 as the dice get cold. By the time you reach that level, you've already pocketed a great deal of profit.

• **Single Odds - Aggressive and Super Aggressive Play**. Let's use a simple rule of thumb here. Add $25 to the $3 game for a single session play, multiply that by three for a day's action. We suggest about $550 for a day's play.

For the $5 game, add $50 to the single session play for a total of $550, and multiply that figure by three for a total of $1,650 for a day's play .

For the single $25 chips play, we need about $1,350 for a single session. Multiply that figure by three for a day's play, and use that guideline for an additional day's play. That comes to $4,050. You can round it off to $4,000.

Triple the above figure for $75 basic bets.

For an extended play bankroll, five times a single session's bankroll will suffice.

2. Double Odds

• **Double Odds - Conservative Play** . With two $5 chips as our basic bet, we still have $30 as our three underlying bets, but our double odds bets raise the overall total to $104. Multiplying that by seven gives us a total of $728. Let's call it an even $700. That makes about $2,000 our necessary bankroll for a day's play.

For the $3 bet, it's $9 on the underlying bets, but $48 for the odds bets, for a total of $57. Multiplying by seven gives us a total of $399. so $350 should be sufficient for a single session. $1,000 is needed for one day's play and an additional $400 for an additional day's play.

With a single $25 chip as our basic bet, we wager $75 as our underlying bets, but must add $220 to that figure as double-odds bets. That comes to $295. Multiplied by seven, it adds up to $2,065. Round it out to $2,000 for a single session. Make it $6,000 for a day's play.

• **Double Odds - Aggressive and Super Aggressive Play**. Let's put our rules of thumb to work again. We'll add $40 to our $3 game for each single session play. That's an additional $100 for the day's play, making a total of $1,100.

For the $10 basic bet, let's add $75 to the single session play and make it $775. A day's play would necessitate about $2,200.

For a $25 bet, we'll increase the session by $125, to $2,125. For the whole day, it's $6,375.

We've left out the ten times odds game in our calculations. Use the same figures as the single $25 game as a basic guide for the ten times game.

Alternate Bankroll Plan

A final note. In calculating all our betting methods bankrolls, we multiplied the single series bets by seven, to give us leverage with our bankroll. However, you can use a multiplication factor of five to have a rock-bottom figure for yourself.

We've multiplied a single session's bankroll by three to get a single day's bankroll, by four to get a bankroll sufficient for two days, and by five to ge an extended stake. This is of course, a worst case scenario if you lose the whole bankroll, which is very unlikely. To again make a rock bottom calculation, use one third the first day's bankroll as a guide for the second day and two-thirds for extended play. Thus, if you need $1,000 for a day's play, you'll need an extra $350 for an additional day's play and $700 for extended play.

In our next section, we'll show you when to leave the table, whether winning or losing, and this will be an additional guide for you and your bankroll.

18. LEAVING THE TABLE

Introduction

One of the best ways to manage your money is knowing when to leave a craps table. Sometimes you'll leave a winner, sometimes a loser. What you should endeavor to do at all times is minimize your losses and maximize your wins. That's by far the best policy.

Limit Losses

Let's assume you've brought $800 to the table. You've been betting with the dice, but nothing has gone right for you. No shooter has made a hot roll. You find you're down about $400. What do you do? In this situation, I might make one more series of bets, and if they didn't turn out well, I'd leave the table. Let's assume the bets cost me $120. Now I'm down $520, but I still have $280 left. I can keep that $280 and take a breather and go to another table later on, starting with this $280.

By the time I've lost $520 I've also lost confidence in the dice. I'm not aggressive, I'm playing a little conservatively. Nothing is going correctly. So, it would seem like the wise move to leave.

However, suppose I feel that the hot roll is overdue. And the dice are coming to me next. I just feel I'll turn things around. In that case I'll stay for my roll. If it fails, I'm gone, losing about another $120.

What I'll never do is this - lose the $800 and then reach for more cash or get more credit. I limit my losses to the single-session bankroll. That's why I devoted so much time to explaining just how much to have at the table for different sized games.

The way to get seduced into putting out more money is when you still have some chips left, but not enough to play out a whole series of rolls without dipping into your pockets. Let's assume each series costs $120. You have $110 in the rails. Leave.

By limiting your losses, you're going to save yourself a lot of grief in the long run. The players who really get hurt are those who permit themselves to take a monster loss, from which they never recover. I've seen this time and time again. It's so frightening a prospect that automatically I'll refuse to let it happen to me.

I've seen players come to Vegas with a bankroll of $6,000 and lose $5,000 at one table, the first table they play at. Then they make a couple of $500 bets to try and raise some cash, and they're flat broke.

If they had lost $800, they'd still have $5,200 as their gambling stake. So don't go crazy. Don't reach for more money after you've lost your session bankroll. And don't ever raise your bets while losing, chasing that elusive dream of quickly getting even. That's the surest way to lose everything.

Only raise your bets when you're winning. We've shown all sorts of systems of betting, conservative, aggressive and super-aggressive. What I like to do is start conservatively, and then move up to aggressive and finally, super-aggressive. Only when I'm winning. When I'm losing, I lay low. I play as conservatively as possible, waiting for that opening, that hot roll to develop. Then I get aggressive.

But I've seen losers do the opposite. If they've been wiped out by a 7, they next double their bets and place all the numbers. Then, after another 7 kills them, they double their bets again, using up all their chips. Then they're gone.

Minimize your losses. Be cautious and conservative when the dice are going against you. Never reach into your pocket or get credit after losing every cent of your table bankroll. If you do these things, you'll do well. You will always have your bankroll ready for the big win.

Another thing. Don't drink while gambling. Don't gamble if you're depressed or unhappy. Gambling isn't a cure for depression; it's playing with fire to gamble when depressed. Play relaxed and with all your wits. That's my advice.

Maximize Wins

We must play to win. That's our only goal. The excitement, fun, thrills of craps should have that one end in mind. To win. Don't play just to have action, just to kill time. Don't play just to have heightened anxiety which you think is excitement. Play to win.

If you are ahead a substantial sum, make certain that you leave the table as a winner. For example, if you're at a $5 table and are ahead by $1,200, leave with at least $800 of it. Set it aside on the rails. The stupidest feeling is to be way ahead and then to lose it all and come out a loser. Don't be stupid. Be a winner.

Sometimes the table keeps going your way. If you're betting wrong, for instance, you get no big wins, but steadily the chips in your rails mount up. Keep it going as long as you can. Let's say you're ahead $400, then $580, then $750, then $920. Slow but steady. Now the dice start to warm up. You count your chips and find you're still up but only by $800. Play out one more series. If you lose, leave. If you win, push that $800 worth of profit to one side, and if you get down there again, leave.

Leave a winner.

If betting right, and you are fortunate to have a hot roll develop while you're at the table, take advantage of that roll. Bet it up, and move from conservative to super-aggressive, all the time taking chips off the table as profit. Let's assume someone has held the dice for fifty-five minutes and during that time your initial bankroll of $800 has gone to $6,500. You're a big winner - $5,700 in profit.

Now the shooter sevens out. The table gives him a good round of applause. He deserved it. What do you do? Leave the table. You're going to get only that one good roll at each session. You got it. Leave at the top. Don't stay there and give back a thousand of the winnings. That thousand will be enough for another session of play somewhere else where another hot roll may occur.

It's hard to set an absolute goal in any game of craps. The game is too dynamic. But keep track at all times of how you're doing. If you've doubled your initial bankroll, that's pretty good. You can leave then and there. Especially if the table has been choppy for the most part, without one clear direction.

If you get tired, if you get tempted to make crazy bets, leave. If you can't think clearly, if you make a couple of stupid mistakes, like not backing up a bet with odds, leave. Go and refresh yourself. Take a long break. The game will be there when you get back. If not that game, there are a thousand others in town.

A final word. You're playing the game with chips, but those chips have a cash value. Just because they're chips doesn't mean you treat them like pieces of clay. Treat them as real money. Just as you wouldn't throw money away, don't make foolish bets. Keep your self-control at all times. If you feel it leaving you, cash in and get away from the table.

With self-control, with money management, with our methods of sane betting only on those wagers that give the house the smallest advantage, you'll have a good chance to win. Craps is a negative game, but keeping the edge of the casino down really low, and with a little luck, and taking advantage of that luck, you can be a winner.

19. HEDGE SYSTEMS

Introduction

I'm going to discuss two systems which have been used to good effect by a discerning craps player I know. Prior to watching him use them, I had never before seen these systems used, and neither had the dealer handling his action. At first, the dealer, a young man in his twenties with the jaded look of someone who had seen everything at the craps table, was amused and dismissive. But as my friend kept pulling chips off the table and as his rails filled up, the dealer began to pay close attention to what he was doing. I'll call my friend John, for purposes of this illustration.

24. Five Bet Reverse System

Here's what John did. He made a pass-line bet of two units and then, after the point was established, he took double odds (all that was allowed at this Strip casino). Then he made a come bet of two units and again took double odds. Then he made another come bet and again took double odds. At this point he had a solid situation, two come bets plus a pass-line wager, all at double odds. The casino only had an edge of 0.6% on all his bets.

But now John kept making come bets. No matter what happened on the table, he made enough come bets to cover four come numbers and one pass-line wager, assuming none of the numbers had repeated. If a number repeated, whether a pass-line or come bet, he kept betting but stopped after five wagers, no matter what happened.

Let's assume the following as his wagers:

Pass-line wager of two units, with a double odds bet backing it up. The point is 4.

A come bet of two units, with a double odds wager backing it up. The first come roll is a 6.

The same with the second come roll, which is a 9.

The same with the third come roll, which is a 10.

The fourth come roll is a 6, and so John got paid off on his first come roll. The 6 is re-established as a come number because of his last come roll.

At this moment in time, John has made one pass-line wager and four come rolls. He has a lot of numbers out there, and if they repeat, he's going to make some good money. If a 7 shows, he's going to lose. What does he do now?

He now makes a sixth wager, but on the don't come, with two units! He reverses his action on the sixth roll of the dice.

A 9 is rolled, and he collects on that come wager, but his new don't come bet is against the dice, on the 9, and he lays double odds against that come point.

He continues to bet on don't come, and the next roll is a 6. Again he collects on the 6, but now has a don't come wager on the 6, with double odds against.

At this moment, here's what his bets look like:

His pass-line bet of 4 still stands, with double odds.

He has a come wager on the 10, with double odds.

He has a don't come wager on the 6 and the 9, both with double odds laid against these points.

He now puts out another two units on don't come. The next roll is his point, 4, and he collects on that wager, but now he has three don't come wagers, with double odds, on the 4, the 6 and the 9. The 10 is hanging there as a come wager.

Now, there's a new come-out roll. But John bets wrong, making a don't pass wager. The new point is 8. He lays double odds, and then, the next roll is a 7. Since he made a don't come wager, he loses two units, but wins all his other don't come bets. If he had just kept betting with the dice, he'd have a slew of come bets, all losers, when the 7 showed its ugly face. But now, he has all winners, except for the 10, which still remained a come wager, and which was lost, along with the odds.

If we assume that his bet was $10, whether right or wrong, here's what he collected on this roll.

On the first repeat of the 6, he collected $34.

On the first repeat of the 9, he collected $40.

On the second repeat of the 6, he collected $34.

On the repeat of the 4, he collected $50.

On the 8 as a don't pass wager, he collected $30.

On the 6 as a don't come wager, he collected $30.

On the 9 as a don't come wager, he collected $30.

Total collections = $248.

He lost $10 on the 7 as a come bet, and $30 on the 10 as a come bet. His total losses were $40, giving him a net win on the roll of $208.

Meanwhile the other bettors, who had bet with the dice, either making place or come bets with odds, lost all their bets when the 7 came up.

The dealer, who had been suspicious of John's strange bets, now nodded his head sagely. I could see he was thinking of trying this method himself the next time he was at the craps table.

I asked John afterwards why he started making don't

come wagers after first making a pass-line and then four additional come bets. He told me that he figured the 7 was bound to come up once every six rolls, and though that wasn't an exact mathematical certainty, he felt uncomfortable after five rolls and started going the other way. He told me he had made some good scores that way.

So, if you want to try it out at home first, to see how well you do, make a pass-line wager and four additional come bets, then start betting don't come, always taking and then giving double odds.

What if you make a pass-line wager, then two come bets, and a 7 comes up? Start again. You'll be surprised, as I was, at the number of times numbers were established and then repeated, and then, after a few don't come wagers, the 7 showed. You win both ways when that happens, and some of these wins can be quite good.

Now, what happens when all the come bets have been replaced with don't come wagers, so that there are only don't come bets on the table? John suggests that you stop betting and wait and see what happens. If you have bad luck, the roll will continue hot and you'll lose most or all of your don't come wagers, but at least you won't be throwing out additional money fighting the roll.

If a situation develops where you have only don't come wagers, and the point bet is still a right bet, and that repeats, then you make one more don't pass wager on the new point and again stop betting.

There are rare instances where the dice are held by a shooter for a long time, where he keeps making numbers, but more often than not, a roll doesn't keep going for a long time. There may be a come wager or two that is repeated, and then the 7 shows. It is these situations that John attempts to take advantage of with his system.

25. The Balancing Act System

This is the name that John picked out for his other system, telling me it amused him to call it that, especially when dealers wanted to know just exactly he was doing.

John's other system involved making a don't pass wager of four units, then laying double odds. After he did this, he made four continuous come wagers of two units with double odds, then stopped. In essence, what he was doing was hedging his come bets with a big don't pass wager. This system worked to perfection on a table where the dice were ice cold, and a 7 would show after the first or second roll.

For example, suppose he bet $20 on the don't pass-line and the point was an 8. He now bet $48 to $40 as a double odds wager against the 8. His next wager was $10 on the come. If a 7 came up, he won the come bet of $10 plus the $60 on the don't pass wager, for a nice $70.

If he made the same wagers, and the point was 8, and the next roll was a 9, he'd place $10 on the 9 as a come bet backed up by $20 on the odds. If the third roll was a 7, he won $10 on the 7, $60 on the 8, and he lost $30 on the 9, for a net win of $40.

What would happen, if after making four come bets, a come bet repeated? He wouldn't make any more wagers. He just wanted come bets to repeat, and if a 7 showed, he felt that his don't pass wager would balance the losses on the table from his come wagers. He was counting on the balancing act coming through for him.

Let's look at a theoretical roll of the dice to see how this worked. After making a four-unit don't pass wager, the point was a 10. He now bet eight units against the 10. If his initial wager was $20 (four $5 units), then he bet $80 to win $40 as double odds.

Now he made a $10 bet on come. The next roll is a 5, and

so he bets $20 on the 5 at double odds.

The next roll is an 8. Having bet $10 on come, he bets $20 as a double odds bet.

The next roll is a 6. He has bet $10 on come, and an additional $20 as a double odds wager.

He now makes his final come wager. A 6 is rolled again, and so he collects $34 on the come point 6.

At this moment in time, he has a $100 wager against the 10, which is the point, and three come bets working, on the 5, 6 and 8.

Let's assume that the next roll is a 3, which is immaterial to him, then an 11, then a 7. Here's what happens now.

He collects $60 for his don't pass wager. He has already collected $34 on the 6, which gives him $94.

He loses $30 on each of the come numbers, 5, 6 and 8, and so he has a paltry net win of $4. When I pointed this out to John, he analyzed what would have happened if he simply made a pass-line wager and four come bets, each $10 with $20 as double odds.

He would have won $34 on the 6, and lost $120 on the point, 10, and the come bets 5, 6 and 8 for a net loss of $86. Also, in the reverse system, he would have lost an additional $10 on the don't come wager, for a net loss of $96. He would have bet don't come since this was the sixth wager to be made.

He informed me that he rarely used this system throughout a whole session of play. He kept with it till the dice warmed up, and found that, at a cold table, he was able to produce some good wins. Then, if a shooter got hot, he found himself switching to the reverse system.

How did he do this? Let's assume that after the shooter made three come numbers, he also made his point. Now, John would bet $10 on the pass-line, re-establish four come numbers or make four come bets hoping to get several come points working, then he would start making don't come wagers.

The one thing John was insistent on was this: he never fought the dice. If the dice were cold, he started off with a big don't pass bet. If the dice got hot, he switched to pass-line wagers and his four come bets, then reversed his field.

Dice work in strange ways, and one can never forecast what they are going to do. John's two systems, which I have called Hedge Systems, tried to move along with the dice. You can try them at home, and see how you like them. I suggest looking at them as another way to try and beat the game of casino dice. The one thing I like about them, as I do about any system, is that at no time are you giving the casino more than 0.6% as its edge.

A final note. John had showed this system to a buddy, who tried to make it come to fruition faster. What he did after making the don't pass wager of four units with double odds against the point, was then to cover all the place numbers other than the don't pass point.

This landed the buddy in deep trouble, because now, instead of simply giving the house a minimum of 0.6% as its advantage, he was giving away from 1.52% to 6.67% to the casino. No one can make money in the long run doing this. John, like other sane craps players had patience; those who believe in shortcuts are going to run into deep trouble.

So, you too, should be patient. Try these systems without using real money at home. If you find that they work, then try them in a casino with small wagers. If they work for you, by all means make bigger bets, but not until you're comfortable and have confidence in them.

20. CRAPS - THE PRIVATE GAME

Introduction

Up to this point, we've discussed the casino game, where a player can bet with or against the dice, and the house will book all his bets. When playing in a casino, there is no such thing as "betting with the house," although players betting don't pass and don't come believe they're doing just that, merely because most players will bet the pass-line. The house has an edge on all line bets, and the casino employees and executives couldn't care less which way a player bets, pass or don't pass.

However, there are so many wagers possible on the craps layout that we concentrated on showing those that are best for a player; that give the house the smallest edge, and in the case of odds bets, give the casino no edge at all.

In the private game of craps, players gamble against each other, without a house or casino booking all bets. The game is similar in that the rules of craps apply, but there are several differences, which will be discussed in full.

How the Game is Played

The private game is usually played in a private setting or something semi-public, such as a garage or loft, depending on how many players are involved. The game can be played anywhere, on the street, in an Army barracks, in a hotel room, you name it and it probably has been played there.

A group of players participate, though the number can be as few as two, or as many as comfortably can fit into the space for the game. I've seen games were there were forty or fifty players all involved in the private game.

Usually, these games, unlike the casino games, are played with cash. That is one big difference. Another is that there is no craps layout. We already discussed the main difference; that there is no house booking all the bets.

The Shooter

One of the participants becomes the shooter. He or she may be chosen by lot or by the roll of the dice, but someone starts off with the dice, holding and shooting them. Before he does so, he puts down cash on the table or floor or the sidewalk; wherever the game is played. Let's say the shooter puts down $100. He now asks to be "faded," that is, have his bet covered. This can be done by one or more individuals.

In a typical game, a player may say, "I'll fade $10," or "I'll cover $10." That still leaves $90 to be faded. Several other players may cover the rest. They do this by putting down their cash on the same surface, in front of them. When they fade or cover the shooter, they are in essence betting wrong, because the shooter always bets with the dice. If the shooter wants to bet against the dice, he must relinquish them.

Let's assume there are eight men participating in a private game of craps. Four have covered the $100 shooter's wager. The other three players can bet with the dice or against the dice, or they may decide not to bet on this particular shoot. Let's assume one of the three players decides to bet with the dice. He puts down $50 in cash and says he's betting with the shooter, and asks to have that amount faded. A player fades only $20 of his bet, and there is no other action. Thus, the player betting the $50 picks up $30 of his wager, leaving the $20 that has been faded.

Let's also assume that another player decides to bet against the dice now. He puts down $40 and announces he's going against the shooter. No one fades any of his wager, so he picks up the $40.

Now the shooter throws the dice. Usually, to insure that the game is level and not fixed, he will throw the dice against a wall or other backdrop, so that the dice will bounce off a solid surface. Let's assume that he rolls a 10. That is now his point.

Odds Wagers

Players can now either lay 2-1 against the 10 as a separate wager, or bet with the dice and get 2-1. Unlike the casino game, players can make odds wagers whether or not they bet with or against the dice initially, and they can wager as much as they want, not dependent upon their original wagers.

This is so, because players are betting against other players, not a casino. After these additional bets are made in cash, everyone knows the point is 10. A 10 coming up on the dice before a 7 will win for all the right bettors and lose for all wrong wagerers; conversely, a 7 showing before a 10 will lose for all right bettors and win for all wrong bettors.

All other numbers showing on the dice are immaterial. There is no layout, so come and place number wagers aren't allowed. It's basically the game of craps reduced to its narrowest level.

The Rules of Private Craps

The shooter's roll determines all wins and losses. He is

always betting with the dice, and those who fade or cover his bets are going against the dice.

If a shooter rolls a 7 or 11 on the come-out roll, he and all those betting with the dice win. If he rolls a 2, 3 or 12 (craps) on the come-out roll, he and all those betting with him lose. There are no barred numbers such as there is at a casino, where either the 2 or 12 is barred to the wrong wagerers.

Any other number, a 4, 5, 6, 8, 9 or 10 becomes the point. Players can make additional or new bets either with the dice or against them, laying or taking the correct odds, which are 2-1 for the 4 and 10, 3-2 for the 5 or 9 and 6-5 for the 6 or 8.

After the odds bets are made, there are generally no other wagers permitted, though any player can decide to increase his odds wager. For example, suppose a player bet $20 against the 10, laying 2-1. After a few more inconsequential rolls, he decides to lay an additional $80 to $40 against the 10. If his bet is faded, he will get action and increase his wager from $20 to $100.

If the shooter makes his point, he continues to hold the dice and he makes a fresh bet that can be faded. If he sevens out, he loses the dice to the next shooter, who now puts down his cash to be faded.

Any player can pass up the dice when it is his or her turn. Some bettors always bet wrong and never want to throw the dice. That is their privilege.

Best Play

Since the 2 or 12 is not barred, the wrong bettor has an advantage of approximately 1.4%, while the right bettor has that disadvantage on his initial wager. Of course, if he makes odds wagers, the right bettor will reduce his disadvantage. For instance, if he makes an odds wager equal to his original bet, it is reduced to 0.8%, and double odds reduces it further to 0.6%. But he still is at a disadvantage.

On the other hand, the wrong bettor keeps an edge no matter what he does in terms of odds wagering. There are other advantages to betting wrong. In sophisticated games, the wrong bettor will have to lay the correct odds on any odds bet, but in many private games, novice gamblers don't really know the correct odds.

Here's a situation that arises quite often. The point is 6 or 8, and a wrong bettor will throw down cash and say, for example, "$50 he doesn't 8." Meaning, he's betting against the point 8 at even-money. He may find some takers, even though he has a 9.09% edge on this wager.

If you find that you can lay even-money on the 6 and 8 as a point, lay as much as you can. You can't get better odds than 9.09% in your favor. But even if you can't get this edge, we still suggest betting against the dice, because of the built-in advantage at the outset.

Craps Terms

In the private game, there are various terms used for certain rolls. "Eighter from Decatur" is used to signify the 8, for example, and the 4 is "Little Joe from Kokomo." 2 is "snake eyes," and so forth.

When a player wishes to bet against the dice or a point, he may say "$30 you don't," rather than "I'm betting $30 against the dice. We already showed how the word "fade" is used to cover another player's wagers.

You never know when you might find yourself in a private game. It's good to know all this information. And of extreme importance - make sure the game is legitimate and the dice aren't crooked. Don't play with a group of strangers, for you may be the one sucker in the game. Play with people you know and trust. And a final note, never play for money if you can't afford to do it either emotionally or financially. That's the best of all advice.

21. GLOSSARY

ADVANTAGE - See **Casino Advantage**

ANY CRAPS - A one-roll wager that the next number coming up will be a 2, 3 or 12.

ANY SEVEN - A one-roll wager that the next number coming up will be a 7.

BACK-LINE - A bet laying odds on Don't Pass or Don't Come.

BAR THE 12 - The barring of the 12 (or 2) as a winning bet for wrong bettors, to ensure that the casino has an edge of those betting against the dice.

BEHIND THE LINE - A bet on the free-odds after a point has been established.

BETTING RIGHT - Wagering that the dice will pass, or win.

BETTING WRONG - Wagering that the dice will not pass, or lose.

BIG 6 AND BIG 8 - A wager, paying even-money that the 6 or 8 will be thrown before a 7.

BOXCARS - A slang expression for the 12.

BOXMAN - A casino executive who sits at the craps table and supervises play.

BRING OUT - A term used by dealers to encourage the players to bet in a certain way, such as a hardway, to *bring* *out* or make the number come up on the dice.

BUCK - The round disk handled by the dealers to show if there is a come-out roll or not, and to show which is the pass-line point, when placed in the appropriate box.

BUY THE 4 OR 10 - To pay a 5% commission to the house in order to get a correct payoff of 2-1 on these place numbers.

CASINO ADVANTAGE - The advantage or edge the house has on any particular bet, or on the game of craps.

CASINO CHECKS - The insider's term for chips used by the casino.

CHANGE COLOR - The changing of casino chips into larger or smaller denominations by the dealer.

CHASING, TO CHASE - Betting large amounts in order to quickly make up a previous loss.

CHIPS - The usual term for the checks issued by a casino in standard amounts, such as $1, $5, $25 and $100.

COLD DICE - Dice that constantly come up with 7s after the shooter establishes a pass-line point.

COME BET - A wager that the dice will pass, or win, made after the come-out roll.

COME BOX - The area on the layout where a Come bet is made by the player.

COME-OUT ROLL - Any roll before a point is established on the pass-line.

CRAPS - 1. The name of the game. 2. Any roll of a 2, 3 or 12.

CRAP OUT - A roll of the dice on the come-out which loses for pass-line and right bettors, when a 2, 3 or 12 shows.

CREW, CREW OF DEALERS - The staff of dealers that run a casino craps game.

CROOKED DICE - Dice that have been altered so that they won't bounce randomly.

DEALER - A casino employee, in house uniform, who handles the players' bets directly, making payouts and collecting losing bets.

DICE - The cubes used in the game, marked with numbers from 1 to 6 as a series of dots.

DIE - A single cube, two of which make up the dice used in the game of casino craps.

DISK - See **Buck.**

DON'T COME BET - A bet made after the come-out roll, betting that the dice will lose.

DON'T COME BOX - The area on the casino layout where a Don't Come bet is made.

DON'T PASS BET - A bet made before the come-out roll that the dice won't pass, or will lose.

DON'T PASS LINE - The area on a casino craps layout where a don't pass bet is made.

DOUBLE ODDS WAGER - A free-odds bet made on Don't Pass, Pass, Don't Come or Come at double the original wager.

EASY, EASY WAY - A roll of a number such as 4, 6, 8 or 10, in which the dice don't show up as pairs, such as 2-2. This is a loser for hardway bettors.

EDGE - See **Casino Advantage.**

EVEN-MONEY PAYOFF - A payout at 1-1.

FIELD BET - A one-roll wager that the next number thrown will be a 2, 3, 4, 9, 10, 11 or 12.

FLOORMAN - A casino executive who approves credit for players and supervises a craps game.

FREE-ODDS BET - A wager made after a point is established on the pass-line or Come, either for or against the dice, at correct odds. The house has no advantage on this bet.

FRONT-LINE - An insider's term for the pass-line.

GEORGE - A Vegas dealer's term for a generous tipper.

HARDWAY BET - A wager that either of the numbers 4, 6, 8 or 10 will come up as pairs before they are thrown easy or a 7 is rolled.

HARDWAYS - Any pair thrown on the numbers 4, 6, 8 or 10.

HIGH ROLLER - A big bettor. Also known as **Premium Player**.

HOP BET - A bet not shown on the layout, where the player wagers that a particular number will come up on the next throw of the dice.

HORN BET - A one-roll wager on the 2, 3, 11 and 12 combined.

HOT HAND - A shooter who is making numbers and winning with his throws is said to have a *hot hand*.

HOT ROLL - A series of throws in which the dice are passing or winning for an extensive period of time.

HOUSE - The entity, also known as the Casino, which books all bets on the craps layout made by the players.

HOUSE ADVANTAGE - See **Casino Advantage**.

INSIDE NUMBERS - The 5, 6, 8 and 9 as point or place numbers.

JUNKET - A group of gamblers who receive complimentary airfare, room and board in return for a certain designated amount of play at certain levels.

LAYOUT - Also known as **Craps Layout**. The imprinted surface of a craps table, showing all the bets that can be made by the players.

LAY THE ODDS - An odds bet, made after a Don't Pass or Don't Come wager, by a wrong bettor, who wagers that a 7 will come up before the number is thrown.

LAY WAGER - A bet against a particular number by a wrong bettor, who gives the casino a 5% commission.

LIMIT - The minimum and maximum betting limits allowed by any particular casino or craps table.

MISS, MISS-OUT - Another term for the shooter sevening-out.

NATURAL - Another term for the 7 or 11 being thrown on the come-out, a winner for pass-line bettors.

NICKELS - A common term for $5 chips.

NUMBERS - The term by gamblers for any of the point numbers - 4, 5, 6, 8, 9 or 10.

OFF - Signifying that certain wagers made by the player will not be affected by the next roll of the dice. For example, place numbers are off on the come-out roll.

OFF-AND-ON - A term used to designate that after a Come bet has been won, and another equal bet is in the Come box, the chips remain where they were, being *off and on*. However, the player is paid for his win.

ON BASE - The term for any standing dealer, to differentiate him from the stickman.

ONE-ROLL BETS - Any bet in which the outcome is determined by the very next roll of the dice.

ON THE STICK - The dealer who is the stickman.

OUTSIDE NUMBERS - The 4, 5, 9 and 10. The 5 and 9 are sometimes considered inside numbers along with the 6 and 8.

PASS - A winning roll for the dice.

PASS-LINE - The area on the layout where pass-line wagers are made.

PASS-LINE BET - A wager made before the come-out that the dice will pass, or win.

PAYOFF - The payment of a winning bet by the dealer.

PIT BOSS - The casino executive in charge of a group of craps tables which constitute a pit.

PLACE NUMBERS, PLACE WAGERS - A bet on either the 4, 5, 6, 8, 9 or 10 as individual numbers or in any combination. The wager is that they will repeat before a 7 is thrown.

PLAYER - A term for the gambler who plays casino craps.

POINT - The numbers 4, 5, 6, 8, 9 or 10 rolled on the come-out or rolled after a Come bet. It becomes the point and must be repeated before a 7 is thrown.

PREMIUM PLAYER -See **High Roller.**

PRESS, PRESS A BET - To increase a bet, usually by doubling it.

PROPOSITION BETS - All the wagers that can be made in the center of the layout.

QUARTERS - Common term for $25 chips.

RAILS - The areas on top of the craps table where players can keep their chips while the game is going on.

RIGHT BETTOR - A gambler who is betting that the dice will pass, or win.

ROLL - The single toss of the dice. Also, a term designating the complete series of throws ending with either a point being repeated or a 7 thrown.

ROLLER - Scc **Shooter.**

SCARED MONEY - Insufficient capital when gambling.

SEVEN-OUT - The rolling of a 7 after a point is established, losing for all right bettors.

SHOOT - A term to designate all the rolls, or series of rolls before a shooter sevens-out.

SHOOTER - The player throwing the dice, whose rolls determine the outcome of all bets on the layout.

STICKMAN - The dealer who controls the dice and the stick, and the center proposition bets. He also calls the gamc.

TAKE DOWN - To remove a bet from the layout, either at the instigation of the player or as a result of the rules of casino craps.

TAKE THE ODDS - An odds bet made by the right bettor, who will receive more than he bets if he wins.

TIP - See **Toke**

TOKE - To give a dealer a gratuity or make a bet for the dealer.

TOM - The Vegas term for a poor toker. As in *Tom Turkey*.

WHALE - The biggest of the high rollers. Someone betting thousands per play at the craps table.

WORKING - A term to describe bets that are subject to being won or lost by the next roll of the dice.

WRONG BETTOR - A player who bets that the dice will lose, or won't pass.

YO-LEVEN -The stickman's slang term for an 11 being rolled.

SAITEK'S GREAT HANDHELD CASINO GAMES!

The World Leader in Intelligent Electronic games

We're stocking these great handheld computer games again! These **exciting palm-sized** games fit into your pockets and can be taken anywhere - they're great travel items! **Easy-to-use**, you'll be playng in just a few seconds. Large LCD screens and superb sound effects bring the excitement and challenge of Las Vegas casino play to you. **High end** line has advance game functions, and streamline designs with lids. Includes automatic five minute powerdown.

PRO BLACKJACK - $39.95

Have fun and learn to win at the same time with this great blackjack computer. Has all the features: choose from 1- 6 deck games, and from 1-3 players at the table. Follows Las Vegas rules and allows $10 to $1,000 bets - hey big spender! Built-in hint key gives advice on all situations and even introduces you to card counting! Has superb casino sounds.

CRAPS PROFESSOR - $79.95

Brand New! The ultimate in craps simulations, this very handsome unit is an electronic trainer *and* game. Follows Las Vegas rules, make all the bets - pass, don't pass, come, don't come, free odds, buy, lay, place and proposition wagers! use electronic dice or roll your own (dice provided). Great casino sounds enhance experience. Comes with comprehensive book, hint cards, and winning strategy cards. Lots of fun!

PRO ROULETTE - $39.95

Beautiful unit has full layout and wheel with all the legal bets plus up to 12 wagers allowing from 1-199 bets! Make any number bet you want, game plays according to the real rules. Even better, up to three can play. Auto power off remembers game; turn on again another time and continue playing. Place your bets, and spin the wheel!!

• •

RADICA'S MONTE CARLO SERIES

From Radica's high-end Monte Carlo series, we've selected these ergonomic and stylish games to keep you in the fun.

3-IN-1 VIDEO POKER COMBO - $39.95

Three games in one; Draw, deuces wild, and loball poker (low hands are winners!)! Random shuffling, realistic payout schedules provides hours of fun!

2-IN-1 SLOT COMBO - $39.95

Las Vegas style slots and European style nudge slots is the closest thing to playing for real. Features 1-5 lines of betting and good action!

BUY ONE OR BUY ALL! GREAT GIFTS!

Yes! I'm ready to play! Buy one or buy all! Enclosed is a check or money order for each game desired (plus postage and handling), made out to:

Cardoza Publishing, P.O. Box 1500, Cooper Station, New York, NY 10276

Call Toll-Free in U.S. & Canada, 1-800-577-WINS

Fax Orders (718)743-8284 - E-Mail Orders: CardozaPub@aol.com

Include $5.00 shipping first game ordered, $2.00 each additional one for U.S; double for Mexico & Canada; HI, AK, other countries 4x. Orders outside U.S., money order payable in U.S. dollars on U.S. bank only.

ITEM DESIRED _____ _____ _____

NAME _____

ADDRESS _____

CITY _____ STATE _____ ZIP _____

Order Today! 30 Day Money Back Guarantee!   CR SP

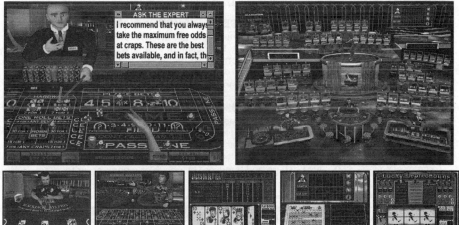